GLORIOUS GLOUCESTERSHIRE

MARK CUMMINGS

The History Press

First published 2024

The History Press
97 St George's Place, Cheltenham,
Gloucestershire, GL50 3QB
www.thehistorypress.co.uk

© Mark Cummings, 2024

British Library Cataloguing in Publication Data.
A catalogue record for this book is available from the British Library.

ISBN 978 1 80399 753 7

Typesetting and origination by The History Press.
Printed and bound in Great Britain by TJ Books Limited, Padstow, Cornwall.

MIX
Paper | Supporting
responsible forestry
FSC
www.fsc.org   FSC® C013056

Trees for Life

CONTENTS

PRAISE FOR *GLORIOUS GLOUCESTERSHIRE*

'I never knew my home county had so many amazing claims to fame. I will enjoy testing friends and family with the 100 local quiz questions. I can't wait to take Mark's advice on how to squeeze every drop out of Gloucestershire.'

Eddie 'The Eagle' Edwards, Olympian.

'I have loved reading about all the legendary characters who have invented, inspired and left amazing legacies. I'm thrilled my dad features amongst many others who have dedicated themselves to keeping Gloucestershire's treasures and traditions thriving.'

Adam Henson, Countryfile presenter.

'A wonderful mixture of history, folklore and local characters. No Gloucestershire home should be without it.'

Katie Fforde, bestselling novelist.

'A brilliant, clever book. Mark Cummings gets it. He understands fully the essence and soul of Gloucestershire and he truly loves it! He is one of us.'

Jack Russell MBE, England cricketer and artist.

'Mark writes just as he broadcasts, with humour and warmth, telling stories about the writers and musicians who have been inspired by our county. I was surprised and intrigued by the stories about Rick Astley, Ivor Novello, Charlie Watts and even Kylie Minogue! Who knew?'

Mike d'Abo, former lead singer of Manfred Mann and composer of 'Handbags and Gladrags' and 'Build Me Up Buttercup'.

'I couldn't wait for Glorious Gloucestershire to be published! I learned so much from Mark's uniquely well-informed, all-encompassing and loving look at the matchless Cotswolds.'

Pam Ayres, poet.

INTRODUCTION

MY GREATEST WISH is that this book will convey my love and emotion for our staggeringly beautiful, innovative and surprising county. I want you to enjoy the wow factor of discovering gems about Gloucestershire you never knew before and feel inspired to explore more profoundly, armed with new knowledge. This is a unique guide, taking both locals and visitors deep into Gloucestershire's soul.

Come with me on a whirlwind journey exploring the Gloucester streets that inspired the characters of Scrooge and Long John Silver, the countryside that gave us Gustav Holst's finest work and the locations where the jet engine, the vacuum cleaner and instant custard were invented. For centuries, Gloucestershire has been at the forefront of innovation and famous historical events, prompting great works of literature and music, and we even have our own rhyming slang. Find out where classic movie scenes were filmed and walk with me to London in the footsteps of Dick Whittington. Fly over the county on Christmas Eve with Santa, discover more about our quirky place names and test your knowledge with the Cummings' County Quiz questions sprinkled throughout the book to help you 'squeeze every drop out of Glorious Gloucestershire'.

This book encapsulates all I have learned and shared over the years with thousands upon thousands of inquisitive, funny, informative radio listeners. After spending thirty years broadcasting with BBC Radio Gloucestershire it is now time to draft my love letter to the county I adore. I am drawing on personal encounters to create something a little bit different. I have spent a year holding the role of the Mock Mayor of Barton, interviewed the real Rosie from *Cider with Rosie* (Rosalind Buckland), created and cycled a 'Tour de Gloucestershire' (200-mile route around the county's iconic locations), hosted guided tours of the Severn bore and looked into the mirror that inspired Lewis Carroll's *Alice Through the Looking-Glass*.

If you are passing through, on a short or long visit, the book will give you a feel for the place and help you explore in a way no other guidebook could. You will definitely return. If you were born here, the book will teach you something you didn't know and you will fall further in love with your county. If you have chosen to move here you will learn so much, so quickly, your relationship and interaction with Gloucestershire will blossom swiftly and your love and connection with the area will enrich your experience of living here.

Gloucestershire feels like one big village connected by five outstanding features: the Forest, the River Severn, the Vale, the Stroud valleys and the Cotswold Hills. Every morning on my BBC Radio Gloucestershire Breakfast Show I felt I could reach out and put my arms right around the county and give it a great big cuddle. We are blessed to have this sense of unity and completeness, as I discovered during storms, floods and the coronavirus pandemic.

I couldn't have written this book without the inspiration and knowledge of my amazing listeners, the patience and skill of my wife, Jo, the support and expertise of the team at The History Press and the help and encouragement of fellow writers and photographers.

I hope you enjoy the ride this book will take you on. As an extra bonus, the purchaser of this book gets their hands on a most sought-after Fern ticket and can act as quizmaster, testing friends and family with a hundred questions about Gloucestershire. Cyclists will have an opportunity to download the route with every twist and turn of my 'Tour de Gloucestershire' ride around the county.

A friend once told me that her mum used to listen to my radio show and loved the way I talked about the county with such affection. She said her heart was so swollen with pride about Gloucestershire that the buttons on her pinny used to pop off. I hope when you finish this book you have no buttons left.

1

BOOK LOVERS' TOUR OF GLOUCESTERSHIRE

IT IS ASTONISHING that in such a small area you can find the inspiration behind so many classic works of iconic literature. Join our exclusive book club and come on a literary journey around the county. We will go through a 'Looking-Glass' and visit places familiar to Dame Jilly Cooper, William Shakespeare and Charles Dickens. We will pop through a magical door into the Dwarven Kingdom, chat about Professor Snape and Humpty Dumpty and even enjoy a refreshing cider with my friend Rosie. We will visit the Gate Streets of Gloucester and step into the worlds of *Peter Pan*, *The Tailor of Gloucester*, *Treasure Island* and *A Christmas Carol*. Our readers' road trip starts with a tipple.

CIDER WITH ROSIE

Our first stop is the Stroud valleys, where we will be immersed in the poetry and prose of the wonderful Laurie Lee. Laurie described the feeling of growing up in the Slad Valley as 'snug, enclosed and protective', and he and his family nestled together like 'peas in a pod'. I had the pleasure of meeting the female inspiration for the famous story *Cider with Rosie*, Rosalind Buckland, who was Laurie's cousin by marriage. She was a twinkly, mischievous, wonderful woman who just happened to be, in her spare time, a literary icon.

We managed to track Rosie down while we were researching a radio show I was planning to present from the Slad Valley. She very kindly granted me an audience and I found myself on her doorstep with a box of chocolates and a bottle of 'you know what'. We discussed sections of the book and explored the picture Laurie painted of growing up in the period just after the First World War. They were all very poor, she remembered, and Laurie's mum was a very strong but kind woman who was always late for everything but was a massive influence on Laurie's life.

Rosalind recalled vivid details of Laurie's two aunties, who always wore long dresses and bonnets. She confirmed how horrible one of their teachers was (the same teacher who was placed on top of a cupboard by a disgruntled student in the book). She told tales of getting a charabanc to Weston for Slad's big day out once a year and the journey taking ages on the old Bristol Road. Winters were extremely harsh as they only had one fire and no central heating.

As for the key episode from the book, what really happened? Laurie describes this pivotal moment with cider-drinking Rosie under a haywain, 'Never to be forgotten, that first long secret drink of golden fire, juice of those valleys and of that time, wine of wild orchards, of russet summer, of plump red apples, and Rosie's burning cheeks. Never to be forgotten, or ever tasted again.' Rosalind told me they were there together in the field but she didn't drink any cider and no funny business went on!

Over time she grew to accept and like the fact that the book was about her, although she hinted that Laurie's accounts were prone to exaggeration. When she grew up she married a policeman and lived in various locations across the county, ending up in Leckhampton. She would occasionally pop over to Slad and meet up with Laurie and she showed me a couple of notes he had given her. One read: 'For Rosie who is never forgotten, Love Laurie.' My favourite, however, is this one: 'To you know who, with long ago love, from you know who ... The author.'

As my time with Rosalind was coming to an end, I produced a bottle of cider from my bag and asked if she would share a glass with me. To our joint amusement she let me have the cider while she stuck with her tea, claiming she didn't really like the stuff and it was a bit early. Just to drink some apple juice with her was a magical moment and it was an interview I will never forget. Maybe if I had stayed a bit later, she might have had a sip of the 'golden fire' because there is a possibility she liked it more than she claimed. Her granddaughter said, 'She always maintained she never drank cider. I got her a bottle of Champagne for her 99th birthday and she said, "Oh, it tastes like cider!" She gave the game away there I think!'

One of my favourite radio interviews
with Rosalind 'Rosie' Buckland.

WHAT THE DICKENS?

Charles Dickens performed on stage at a theatre on Gloucester's Westgate Street during a reading tour and described Gloucester as 'a wonderful and misleading city'. He was fond of nearby Cheltenham, 'I have rarely seen a place that so attracted my fancy.' Tewkesbury also caught his eye and it was mentioned in *The Pickwick Papers* when Mr Pickwick and his friends stop at a coaching inn, the Hop Pole, on their way from Bristol to Birmingham. 'At the Hop Pole, Tewkesbury, they stopped to dine, upon which occasion there was more bottled ale, with some Madeira and some port besides ... and here the case bottle replenished for the fourth time.' Now that's my idea of a good lunch. One final link that might surprise you is in the heart of the Cotswolds at Bibury, known for its Trout Farm and historic chocolate box cottages at Arlington Row. A short walk from the main village is the fabulous Bibury Court Hotel. I have been to wedding receptions and long lunches here, but I didn't know until recently that there is a Dickensian link. This Jacobean manor was formerly owned by the Cresswell family and it is thought to have been their long-running dispute over a family will that inspired the court case in *Bleak House*.

SCROOGE

Since Charles Dickens was a regular visitor to Gloucester, it is widely accepted that he based his character Scrooge on his knowledge of the local banker James 'Jemmy' Wood. Jemmy was a well-known miser who ran the bank on Westgate Street and became known as 'the richest commoner' in England. He was born in 1756 and inherited a shop and bank from his father. Over the years he made a mint but was unpopular with the locals because of the way he conducted his business. He was a shabby character who never spent any money on clothes and was known to go to the nearby Gloucester Docks to pick up pieces of coal from the barges moored there. He was too mean to pay for transport, so would walk huge distances. He was once walking back from Tewkesbury in the rain when he eventually accepted a lift from a hearse. He climbed into the back and sat next to the coffin. When he died he left around £50 million in today's money but his coffin was pelted with stones and the crowds booed during his funeral procession. He is buried in St Mary de Crypt Church in Gloucester.

If you keep these descriptions in mind, you will appreciate the similarities between Jemmy Wood and Dickens's descriptions of Scrooge. 'The cold within him froze his old features, nipped his pointed nose, shriveled his cheek, stiffened his gait; made his eyes red, his thin lips blue and spoke out shrewdly in his grating voice.' A few years ago, I met a distant relative of Jemmy Wood. He joined us on a procession through the city on Gloucester Day and was utterly charming. We took him to the pub afterwards, had several rounds of drinks and, interestingly, he never paid for single one.

Jemmy Wood. (Gloucester Civic Trust)

LONG JOHN SILVER AND W.E. HENLEY

William Ernest Henley was born near Gloucester Cross at 5 Eastgate in 1849 and spent nearly half of his life in this city centre location. This man has always fascinated me because of the huge impact he had in many literary areas despite his own physical suffering and the loss of his daughter at a very young age. We are so proud that this poet, editor and critic was born in our county. Shortly after starting at the Crypt Grammar School he was attacked by tuberculosis of the bone, an illness that plagued him all of his life. He was only a teenager when his left leg was amputated below the knee. In a search for a cure, he was admitted in his early twenties to the Edinburgh Infirmary in 1873. It was here that he met and became close friends with Robert Louis Stevenson. They were nearly the same age, both were writers and they were fighting the same disease. Henley had a big, loud personality and a gingery beard, and when Stevenson wrote his first novel, *Treasure Island* in 1883, he based one-legged Long John Silver on his good friend. He wrote to Henley, 'It was the sight of your maimed strength and masterfulness that begot Long John Silver … the idea of the maimed man, ruling and dreaded by the sound, was entirely taken from you.'

There is a blue plaque dedicated to Henley at Gloucester Cross where the four Gate Streets meet with a quote from his famous poem 'Invictus', written in 1875.

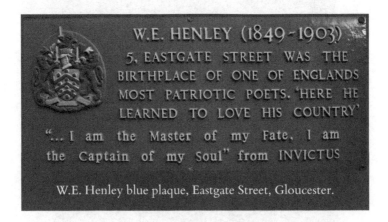

W.E. Henley blue plaque, Eastgate Street, Gloucester.

It is thought the inspiration for the poem came from his struggles with his health and loss of his leg. His motivational words inspired the title of the 2009 film about the South Africa rugby team's bid to win the Rugby World Cup, and Nelson Mandela famously recited the poem to his fellow prisoners while he was in prison on Robben Island.

Invictus

Out of the night that covers me,
Black as the pit from pole to pole,
I thank whatever gods may be
For my unconquerable soul.

In the fell clutch of circumstance
I have not winced nor cried aloud.
Under the bludgeonings of chance
My head is bloody, but unbowed.

Beyond this place of wrath and tears
Looms but the Horror of the shade,
And yet the menace of the years
Finds and shall find me unafraid

It matters not how strait the gate,
How charged with punishments the scroll,
I am the master of my fate,
I am the captain of my soul.

PETER PAN'S WENDY

W.E. Henley's daughter, Margaret, was the inspiration for Wendy Darling, J.M. Barrie's character in *Peter Pan*. Barrie and Henley were good friends and would often meet up. Sadly, Margaret was a poorly child, unable to speak clearly, and she referred to Barrie as her 'fwendy-wendy'. This amused and inspired Barrie, who coined the name Wendy for his famous character. Although Margaret had a short life, having died aged 5 of cerebral meningitis, she is immortalised in the classic *Peter Pan*.

J.M. BARRIE

Stanway House brings out two very different reactions in me. The first one is when I am cycling past and I have to face the impending horror of cycling up the never-ending Stanway Hill. The second is more pleasant as it is a lovely memory of spending a dreamy afternoon there with David Carroll, the author of *A Literary Tour of Gloucestershire and Bristol*. His love of literary connections was infectious and lit a spark in me. Stanway House takes your breath away with its magical gatehouse, tiny church, fourteenth-century tithe barn, water gardens and the 300ft single-jet fountain, the highest gravity fountain in the world. You can understand why J.M. Barrie fell in love with this place and rented it for six weeks every summer from 1921 to 1932. His cast list of summer house guests was impressive, including Sir Arthur Conan Doyle, Walter de la Mare and H.G. Wells. David told me guests were encouraged to indulge in Barrie's love of cricket and would spend many an afternoon at the village cricket club. Apparently, the rule was not to get Barrie out and to let him bat for as long as he wanted. The local cricket pavilion was an old railway carriage but Barrie wanted to leave a gift for the village so he designed and paid for a lovely thatched pavilion as a replacement. Stanway House has its own chapel and rumour has it that the tiny character on the weathervane on the roof was the inspiration for Tinker Bell, the fairy in *Peter Pan*. I would so love this to be true, but my friend David spoilt my fantasy by showing me the dates. Sadly, they don't add up – Barrie had already written *Peter Pan* before his visits to Stanway House.

THE 'TRAMP POET' W.H. DAVIES

There is a magical zigzaggy road full of breathtaking sharp bends that drops from Minchinhampton Common into the town of Nailsworth in the Stroud valleys. It is called the Nailsworth W, has an eye-wateringly steep gradient and I cycle this challenging route quite often. As I see the rooftops and chimneys of Nailsworth appear beneath me, I without fail quote out loud:

> What is this life if full of care,
> We have no time to stand and stare.

I do this because the man who wrote the poem 'Leisure' used to live at the bottom of the Nailsworth W. After a death-defying descent down this magnificent road there is a right turn to a place called Watledge, where the poet William Henry Davies spent his last years. He was known as the 'tramp poet' because in his early twenties he left his home in Wales and travelled through America as a homeless person, spending time in various jails. His life on the road ended in a horrible way when he lost his right leg in an accident while jumping from a train. Back in this country, he wrote poetry and his big break came when the poet Edward Thomas publicly supported his work and gave him the confidence to write his famous *Autobiography of a Super-Tramp* in 1908. Having spent many years in London, he eventually moved to Gloucestershire and settled in Nailsworth. He lived in various properties around the town, ending up in Glendower, a small two-storey cottage with an elevated view over town. He clearly loved this location, which featured in his poem 'Nailsworth Hill':

> The moon that peeped as she came up
> Is clear on top with all her light.
> She rests her chin on Nailsworth Hill,
> And, where she looks, the world is bright.

'Tramp poet' W.H. Davies's cottage Glendower
at Watledge overlooking Nailsworth.

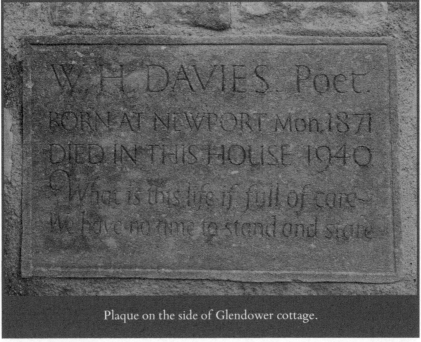

Plaque on the side of Glendower cottage.

Davies died in 1940, leaving a legacy of work that endures to this day. Here is a fascinating fact you can casually weave into a conversation: what is the link between W.H. Davies and an iconic rock band? The band Supertramp took their name from Davies's *Autobiography of a Super-Tramp*. In the early years before any commercial success the band was originally called 'Daddy', but they needed to change their name as there was another band around at the time called 'Daddy Longlegs'. The name change was inspired by their love of the work of our 'tramp poet'.

The company Center Parcs has used the opening lines of the famous poem 'Leisure' in its TV adverts. I have a wooden plaque in my wild flower garden inscribed with the same first two lines.

Leisure

What is this life if, full of care,
We have no time to stand and stare?
No time to stand beneath the boughs,
And stare as long as sheep and cows:
No time to see, when woods we pass,
Where squirrels hide their nuts in grass:
No time to see, in broad daylight,
Streams full of stars, like skies at night:
No time to turn at Beauty's glance,
And watch her feet, how they can dance:
No time to wait till her mouth can
Enrich that smile her eyes began?
A poor life this if, full of care,
We have no time to stand and stare.

DAME JILLY COOPER – SEARCHING FOR PARADISE

Dame Jilly has lived in the dreamy village of Bisley for more than four decades and Gloucestershire has inspired much of her work. I have had the joy of spending time with her in her stunning house nestled above Stroud, usually talking about our shared love of rescued lurchers. I think we can safely assume *Polo* and *Riders* had something to do with the horsey county that became her home. Gloucestershire is awash with royalty, high society, show jumping legends and classic polo events in places such as Cirencester and Westonbirt. Dame Jilly's novel *Tackle* was loosely based on her local football team, Forest Green Rovers. She is a dedicated fan and I know the club are thrilled to have her support. My favourite story about Dame Jilly centres on her novel *The Man Who Made Husbands Jealous*.

Celebrating with Dame Jilly Cooper
at an awards ceremony.

The main character, Lysander Hawkley, makes a good living from help-ing lonely housewives feel better about themselves (if you get my drift), which in turn is meant to encourage their husbands to appreciate them more. Dame Jilly's choice of name for the village where all this 'action' took place was Paradise. However, Dame Jilly hadn't realised that there is an actual place in Gloucestershire called Paradise only a few miles from Bisley. I remember at the time the *Daily Mirror* sent a reporter to this tiny hamlet near Painswick to try and find a local Lothario who might have inspired Dame Jilly's 'racy' blockbuster. I interviewed her and she was equally embarrassed and amused at her 'blooper'.

THE TAILOR OF GLOUCESTER

If you visit No. 45 Westgate Street in Gloucester, it will probably be a pub now. The names have changed over the years but its usage has always been a meeting place for a decent drink and a lively chat. In the late 1880s, however, it was the workplace of Mr Prichard, the real-life tailor of Gloucester. The story that inspired Beatrix Potter to write her children's book *The Tailor of Gloucester* goes a bit like this: Mr Prichard was commissioned to make a waistcoat for the new mayor of the city to wear at his first official function, leading a procession from the Guildhall on Eastgate Street all the way down to Shire Hall on Westgate Street. At this particular time, Mr Prichard was snowed under with work and on the Saturday before the procession he had gone home leaving the waist-coat, still unfinished, lying on a workbench. When he came back on the Monday morning he found that the waistcoat had been completed apart from one buttonhole. He was thrilled that his assistants had finished off the waistcoat for him. They left a note against the unfinished buttonhole, saying 'No more twist!' The tailor decided this was an opportunity to create a fun story so attributed the help to a group of kind fairies. He put a notice in his shop window explaining his theory and hence the legend was born. When Beatrix Potter heard the tale, she was inspired to write her story, but she changed the fairies to mice.

BEATRIX POTTER

Potter's connection with the area started with a visit in 1894 to some relatives, the Huttons, who lived near Stroud. She was very close to her cousin Caroline, who told her about the tale of the local tailor, Mr Prichard. Beatrice went to 45 Westgate Street and also sketched some of the stunning buildings leading to Gloucester Cathedral, including 9 College Court. This magical lane links Westgate Street with College Green and was the setting in Potter's mind for *The Tailor of Gloucester*. No. 9 College Court is now a museum full of books, gifts and collectables but don't be fooled: the building where the tailor Pritchard lived is thirty seconds away back on Westgate Street.

J.K. ROWLING

Gloucester Cathedral was once used as a location for the filming of the *Harry Potter* franchise, but J.K. Rowling's connection with Gloucestershire runs far deeper. She was born in Yate in South Gloucestershire in 1965. The family moved to Church Cottage in Tutshill in 1974, which is just inside Gloucestershire as you climb the hill out of Chepstow. She went to Wyedean School in Sedbury near the Severn Bridge. During her teens she was head girl and characters such as Snape and Ron Weasley are said to be based on teachers and friends from that time. Former teachers have spoken openly about which elements of the school they think made it into the books. The house structure at Hogwarts was an integral element of Wyedean with huge competition between houses. Sport was seen as a vital way of building character. The late Head of Chemistry, John Nettleship, is universally thought to be the inspiration for the potions master, Professor Snape. He had a big nose and long dark hair and could be quite strict. At first, he apparently didn't like the comparison, but soon got used to it and embraced the idea when his colleagues, friends and family all became convinced he was Snape. Rowling has subsequently bought her childhood home and has upgraded the Grade II listed stone cottage, where she once wrote on a window frame 'Joanne Rowling slept here circa 1982'.

One final link takes us to the market town of Dursley near Stroud, which is not far from Yate. Rowling's muggle family, with the surname Dursley, are Harry Potter's only known living close relatives. Rowling described them as 'reactionary, prejudiced, narrow-minded, ignorant and bigoted'. At first many of us thought she had used the name for these unpopular characters because she didn't like the town itself. The rumour persisted for years and many of us felt sorry for the people of the town because it is a lovely, down to earth, historic place with a fabulous, warm community. Thankfully, the author cleared up any confusion a few years later when she said, 'I have never visited Dursley, and I expect that it is full of charming people. It was the sound of the word that appealed rather than any association with the place.'

J.R.R. TOLKIEN

If you love the work of Tolkien, there are plenty of great locations in Gloucestershire to fire your imagination. Let's begin in the east at St Edward's Church in Stow-on-the-Wold. Take a close look at the church's north door, which is flanked by two ancient yew trees with a lantern hanging above. This is thought to have inspired the door to the Dwarven kingdom of Khazad-dûm (Moria) and might explain why hordes of Tolkien addicts have turned up at the church to command 'Gate of the Elves, open now for me'. Stow was one of Tolkien's favourite places to visit when he was Professor of English down the road at Merton College in Oxford. Rumour has it that he enjoyed the nearby pubs in Moreton-in-Marsh and the Bell Inn is said to have inspired the Prancing Pony where Gandalf enjoyed a tipple.

Let's head to west Gloucestershire now and explore Tolkien's time spent in the Forest of Dean. In 1929 he worked on an ancient archaeological site at Lydney Park, which is the site of an old Roman temple known as Dwarf's Hill and an earlier Iron Age settlement. Locals believed dwarves and hobgoblins lived in the area. You can't blame Tolkien for allowing Lydney Park with its tunnels and mines to influence his thinking and writing. If you keep heading west you come to the magical Puzzlewood and it is a wondrous experience to wander around this enchanting and mysterious woodland. I had a private tour

Entrance to St Edward's Church,
Stow-on-the-Wold.
(Cotswolds Tourism, Cotswolds.com)

at dusk once and was left alone to find my way out! It is often described as Tolkienesque and many locals are convinced this was the inspiration for Middle Earth in *The Lord of the Rings*.

SHAKESPEARE IN GLOUCESTERSHIRE

If you pop into the gift shop at Tewkesbury Abbey, be sure to pick up some Tewkesbury mustard. It comes in the form of a mustard ball wrapped in mock gold leaf. It will have two immediate effects on you.

Firstly, it will put hairs on your chest; and secondly, you will spend the rest of the day reciting Shakespearian quotes uncontrollably. In *Henry IV*, Falstaff describes Poins as having 'a wit as thick as Tewkesbury mustard'. This pungent mixture of crushed mustard seeds spiced up with local horseradish would have been familiar to Shakespeare's audiences as it was sent all over the country. It was thick and smelly and is still being made today.

This is one of many Shakespearian quotes linked to Gloucestershire and so many references to the county could lead us to speculate that the great man might once have lived among us. My friends in Dursley certainly think so. In *Richard II*, the Earl of Northumberland says, 'I am a stranger here in Gloucestershire. These high wild hills and rough uneven ways draws out our miles.' Many claim Shakespeare was describing the view from the top of Stinchcombe Hill, looking down on to Berkeley Castle, when he wrote 'there stands the castle by yon tuft of trees' and believe it was drawn from local knowledge he would only have known if he had lived there.

In *Titus Andronicus*, Marcus says 'it would rouse the proudest panther', and apparently 'panther' is a southern Cotswold word for a poet.

In *Henry IV*, Davy says, 'I beseech you, sir, to countenance William Visor of Woncot against Clement Perkes o' th' hill.' Apparently, Woodmancote was known as Woncot or Womcot or Wincott, and Stinchcombe Hill was known locally as 'the hill', while a house on Stinchcombe Hill belonged to a Purchas or Perkis family. The Vizard or Visor family lived in Woodmancote and one of them was bailiff of Dursley in 1612. In the woods between Woodmancote and Stinchcombe Hill there is a path that was known as 'Shakespeare's walk' until relatively recently.

EVELYN WAUGH

Author Evelyn Waugh moved to Stinchcombe, which he referred to as 'Stinkers', in 1937 and lived in the impressive Grade II listed Piers Court, as well as becoming president of the Dursley Dramatic Society. It was during this time that he wrote *Brideshead Revisited*.

EDWARD THOMAS

Adlestrop is a few miles from Stow-on-the-Wold and it is well worth a visit for poetry lovers and those who appreciate a delicious moment of tranquillity. Prior to Mr Beeching and his cuts, Adlestrop had a small, picturesque Cotswold railway station, which was the inspiration for the classic poem 'Adlestrop' by Edward Thomas, thanks to a journey he took in June 1914. The train briefly stopped here and Thomas's words describing peaceful, rural Gloucestershire contrast starkly with the imminent outbreak of the First World War. Tragically, Thomas was killed in action in 1917, just before the poem was due to be printed.

IVOR GURNEY

Gloucester musician and poet Ivor Gurney was a huge fan of Edward Thomas and set some of his poetry to music. Unlike his friend, he survived the war. 'Severn and Somme' was the first of Gurney's war poems and he later explained that while writing it, surrounded by sights and sounds of war, he was thinking of his aching love for Gloucestershire. Reading the poem puts a huge lump in my throat and also makes me exhale with longing for Gloucestershire. I urge you to read this poem that mentions Framilode, Redmarley, May Hill and the Severn.

The view that inspired Ivor Gurney's yearning for the Severn and May Hill from the trenches.

HUMPTY DUMPTY

Humpty Dumpty sat on the wall,
Humpty Dumpty had a great fall;
All the king's horses and all the king's men
Couldn't put Humpty together again.

There are two theories about Gloucester's claim on this famous nursery rhyme. One theory is that Humpty Dumpty was a drink of brandy boiled with ale, and the term may relate to a local who was unable to hold their booze and would wobble around before collapsing. Another theory suggests Humpty Dumpty originated from the name of a cannon used during the Siege of Gloucester in 1643.

LEWIS CARROLL'S LOOKING-GLASS

As I once entered a rather grand house, Hetton Lawn, at Charlton Kings on the outskirts of Cheltenham, my stomach was fluttering with butterflies. I knew at the top of the stairs I would be staring into an iconic mirror that could lead into a magical and strange world. The large, ornate over-mantel mirror at Hetton Lawn is thought to date from the early 1860s. It is huge and when you stare into it you can appreciate why it had such an impact on the Reverend Charles Lutwidge Dodgson, or Lewis Carroll as most of us know him.

Gloucestershire claims to be the inspiration behind Carroll's *Through the Looking-Glass*, and the girl who falls down a hole into a magical world is believed to be based on Alice Liddell. Her father, Dr Henry Liddell, the Dean of Christ Church College in Oxford, was a friend of Lewis Carroll and her grandparents lived at Hetton Lawn. Carroll used to take Alice and her sisters Lorina and Edith on boat trips and picnics, and during these adventures he would tell them stories that became the inspiration for *Alice's Adventures in Wonderland* and *Through the Looking-Glass*. Carroll visited the siblings while they were staying with their grandparents at the house with the ornate mirror.

Carroll's Cheltenham visit also prompted another of his famous characters. During a walk with Alice at Leckhampton Hill, Carroll met her school governess, Miss Prickett. He described her as being 'the quintessence of all governesses' and she inspired the character of the Red Queen in *Through the Looking-Glass*. Carroll even referred to Hetton Lawn, the house at Charlton Kings, as 'the Looking-Glass House'.

Looking-Glass mirror at Hetton Lawn, Charlton Kings. (David Elder)

How to Squeeze Every Literary Drop Out of Glorious Gloucestershire

Walk along the Gate Streets in Gloucester, starting at the Cross where all four streets merge. Here, on Eastgate Street, you will find a blue plaque dedicated to W.E. Henley. Head down Westgate Street and look out for 'Scrooge's' workplace on your right, currently a McDonald's. On your left you will see the original Tailor of Gloucester's house before you turn right along College Court to find The House of the Tailor of Gloucester Museum and shop. The brilliant Gloucester Civic Trust provide fabulous walking tours from April to September and give private tours all year round on request.

For a proper Laurie Lee experience, I suggest three simple activities: Enjoy the food and drink in the Woolpack pub in Slad and sit in Laurie's favourite seat. Then head over the road to the church where Laurie is buried and find his gravestone. He famously said he wanted to be buried overlooking his favourite pub so that 'I can balance the secular with the spiritual'. Finally, immerse yourself in the valley by completing a simple 5-mile walk, the Laurie Lee Wildlife Way. Look out for the ten strategically placed wooden 'poetry posts' that allow you to imbibe the spirit of this wonderful man.

If you want to let your hair down and find out more about Dame Jilly Cooper's Gloucestershire then check out a polo match at Cirencester Park Polo Club or the Beaufort Polo Club at Westonbirt. Perhaps you would like to go on a voyage to discover Paradise? If so, take the A46 out of Painswick towards that world-famous cheese-rolling Coopers Hill and it is on your right. While you are there you must pop into the Painswick Rococo gardens.

Shakespeare fans must go to Dursley and explore claims that he lived there. Ask the locals to fill you in. Then head off to the top of Stinchcombe Hill and try to locate Berkeley Castle in the distance.

Fans of both Dickens and Shakespeare should spend a day in Tewkesbury. Pop into any gift shop and get yourself a ball of Tewkesbury mustard. Consume it in any way that works for you, then head over to the Royal Hop Pole pub to calm your mouth down.

A visit to J.M. Barrie's summer retreat is another must. Stanway House is open in June, July and August and appeals to all ages with its magical water gardens, world-famous gravity fountain and stunning house. While in the area why not book at trip on the Gloucestershire Warwickshire railway five minutes away at Toddington?

To celebrate the work of Ivor Gurney simply find anywhere with a view of both the River Severn and May Hill. That is all you need, then simply read 'Severn and Somme'.

For pure relaxation, jump in the car, pop some Supertramp on and head to Nailsworth. With the poem 'Leisure' flowing through your veins, take the short walk up to Watledge (first left after the cattle grid) and look for the cottage called Glendower. Then find somewhere in this magical town to simply 'stand and stare'.

I suggest fans of *The Hobbit* and *The Lord of the Rings* take a couple of days over the following ideas. Spend a day in the North Cotswolds exploring Tolkien's favourite haunts: St Edward's Church in Stow-on-the-Wold is a must. Locate the north door and gaze into another world. You might need a drink after that, so head a few minutes up the road to Morton-in-Marsh and seek out Tolkien's favourite pub.

Harry Potter fans, Gloucester Cathedral is the place for you.

CUMMINGS' COUNTY QUIZ

ROUND ONE

1. True or false? Stroud-based singer-songwriter Mike d'Abo wrote the hit 'Build Me Up Buttercup', but is it true that when he offered the song to David Essex he turned it down because he didn't want to sing a song about a cow?

2. What is the glorious arboretum near Moreton-in-Marsh called?

3. Where would you find the famous Bulls Cross? It features in a literary classic.

4. Which has the biggest population, Dursley or Bishop's Cleeve?

5. Which queen is said to have hunted with her lord in the woods near Painswick shortly before her death?

6. What is the county flower of Gloucestershire?

7. Which Cotswold village was described by William Morris as 'the most beautiful in England'?

8. In which famous Forest of Dean building would you find the Verderers' Court Room?

9. Is Strensham in or out of Gloucestershire?

10. Which of the following places do not exist in Gloucestershire: Knockdown, Ready Penny, Bertie's Bottom?

2

GOURMET GLOUCESTERSHIRE

I THINK IT is time to make you salivate at the prospect of squeezing every drop out of Gloucestershire's delicious food and drink heritage. Come with me on a scrumptious roller coaster ride as we gobble down a Gloucester Dripper, catch and cook elvers, indulge in some local celebrity chef gossip – and my big scoop is exclusive stories of what really happened on the Wall's ice cream factory floor.

Every October I watch on in awe at the *Cotswold Life* Food and Drink Awards celebrating the farmers, producers, restaurateurs, chefs, pubs, cafés, cake shops, delis, brewers, bakers and butchers of this incredible area. Some previous winners include: Cotswold Gold rapeseed oil, Cherry Moo luxury handmade ice cream and Hobbs House Bakery. Other food heroes who have helped put the county at the forefront of the UK gastronomic map include Stroud Farmers Market, the innovative Harts Barn Cookery School and the Foraging Course Company, who have a base in North Cerney.

Let's dive into a smorgasbord of other Gloucestershire tasty treats.

ELVERS

Lovable rogue Hartley Everett was the quintessential elver fisherman, a hilarious storyteller and my friend. He knew how to extract every morsel out of the River Severn and taught me everything I need to know about elvers. He also told me in no uncertain terms what used to happen to rival fisherman who invaded his 'tump' (his exclusive prime spot for catching these wriggly little blighters). These ugly-looking eels used to be plentiful and a staple in the Gloucestershire diet until stocks ran low, and now they are a rare and expensive delicacy. You either love them or hate them. I like to cook them in the rind of Gloucester Old Spot bacon but some like them mixed into scrambled egg and others add onions and herbs. If you walked down the street and a house had a dining chair outside the front door with a tea towel on the back of it, that was the signal that they had elvers for sale. They would usually be kept in a tin bath. To this day there is still an elver eating competition at the Frampton Country Fair, although now they use a sustainable Spanish alternative made from elver-shaped surimi fish paste, known affectionately as 'el-vers'. Eating them with Hartley outside his house at Longney Crib looking out over the River Severn towards the Forest of Dean was one of life's great privileges.

Elver Hartley Everett by his beloved River Severn.

ICE CREAM

Gloucestershire has a deep and enduring love of the world of ice cream. My daughters are now grown up but they still excitedly scan the horizon on Minchinhampton Common hoping the Winstones ice cream van will be there. It is part of who we are and here are some past and present local names to get you licking your lips: Wall's, Wholly Gelato, Tartaglia, Winstones, De Tomaso, Boselli, Cherry Moo and so many more. The emotional connection runs deep with this delicious, indulgent treat, so here are some thoughts from listeners who called my radio show.

Many remembered the Italian Tartaglia family, who were famous for their cider lollies and often provided local schools with free goodies on feast days. The De Tomaso dynasty also came from Italy and their 'stop me and buy one' offer still takes a 70-year-old listener straight back to their childhood! Many people in the area with the family name Thomas have a tutti frutti family secret. They might have lost the full Italian moniker but don't be fooled, they have raspberry ripple pumping through their veins.

At the Wall's factory in Gloucester, 200 Viennettas are made every minute and 4 million Cornettos are constructed every week. Many of my listeners shared the most wonderful stories about their connections with the company. Pat remembered the day they had a 'full freezer' issue at the factory so she came home with a dozen 1-litre tubs of Belgian Chocolate, which filled her freezer, her sister's freezer and her neighbour's freezer. Rebecca worked next door at the Barclays Data Centre and remembers when they brought out the Cornettos; the smell of the waffle cones baking was torment for the shift workers finishing at midnight. Jane's job was to show guests around the factory and she once gave Ken Dodd a tour, while Tom's greatest memory was showing Queen Elizabeth II all the machines and gadgets (she apparently loved a Viennetta). Mike's uncle John worked at Wall's and he will never forget the day he brought one of the first ever Viennettas home for Sunday tea, making them all feel so posh. I agree, it was the same for us, and even to this day I feel we are pushing the boat out when we demolish one for pudding. Another former employee, Chris, told me that when he first started, the service road came out onto the Wall's roundabout and you had to queue for ages on a Friday just to get out on your way home.

The classic Wall's 'stop me and buy one' trike.

Wall's ice cream factory floor.

He used to make a Dracula ice cream that turned his hands green. Stan reminisced about his dad, who cycled many miles on his trike delivering ice cream for Wall's. His most tiring journey took him from Gloucester all the way to Cranham.

MENU OF OTHER LOCAL DISHES

Here is a little menu card with some other Gloucestershire delicacies you might want to try for the first time or recreate. The first is the Gloucester Pancake, guaranteed to put hairs on your chest. This isn't just any kind of pancake, it is a monster full of lard and sugar. A cross between a doughnut and a Welsh cake, it is not for the faint-hearted. Other gourmet Gloucestershire grub includes pork chops smothered in Double Gloucester cheese and horseradish; lamprey pie, which is a rather disgusting fish dish traditionally made for the queen; the famous dripper, which is our version of lardy cake; Blaisdon plumb jam sandwich; a type of hot pot called a Painswick bow-wow pie (so called because of a myth that locals served dog meat at an annual town ceremony); and finally chicken in a basket, which was first served this way at the Mill at Withington and the pub reserves the right to claim the concept.

FANCY A TIPPLE?

If you have now developed a thirst, don't worry, Gloucestershire can help you with that. We are famed for our award-winning local breweries and vineyards and world-renowned gin distillers. Most weeks you can find a cracking beer festival, and never forget our native ciders and perry perfection. This might have something to do with our West Country heritage and the characters who have played a major role in it. If, in times gone by, you fancied a glass or two of rough home-made cider, Jasper Ely was your man. Jasper was a water bailiff (a type of water policeman) and one of the River Severn's great characters. I have been told he would have two pints at 4 a.m., do his rounds, and then be back for another two pints with bacon and eggs for breakfast!

CHEESE BOARD

When you put the words 'Gloucestershire' and 'cheese' together, one crazy, death-defying image comes to mind: a huge Double Gloucester hurtling down Coopers Hill followed by a raggle taggle band of nincompoops chasing the wheel of wonder. Diana Smart used to make the cheese for the May madness and when I interviewed her I felt I was chatting to cheese royalty. She was a farmer in Churcham and only started making cheese in her sixties, determined to make the most traditional local cheeses she could. The family have carried on the tradition and Smart's Traditional Gloucester Cheese operates from the same farm in Churcham. The Gloucester cheeses came close to extinction in the twentieth century, which is where cheese maker and conservationist Charles Martell comes in. He was instrumental in saving them when, in the

Charles Martell.

1970s, he decided to preserve the Old Gloucester cattle breed that would originally have been used, and began to make both Single and Double Gloucester cheeses. The Single Gloucester style is now a 'PDO' cheese (Protected Designation of Origin). The status was gained in 2007 and it means that the cheese has to meet a specific list of characteristics in order to merit the name. Charles also produces the intoxicating Stinking Bishop, named after the pear used to make the perry that the cheese is washed in during the maturing process. The world became aware of our smelly Gloucestershire secret in 2005 when Gromit used it to revive Wallace in the film *The Curse of the Were-Rabbit*. Demand went crazy and Charles had to hire more staff to cope.

SAUCY TIMES WITH TOM

Tom Kerridge is a famous chef, TV star and author. He is just as funny and lovely in real life as he is on the telly, and he is ours. I have inter-viewed Tom many times and here is an amuse-bouche of delicious anecdotes: he grew up in a single-parent family in Matson in Gloucester and happily admits to being one of the 'naughty boys'. He used to attend drama classes at the Everyman Theatre in Cheltenham, mainly because the girls from Cheltenham Ladies College always liked a 'naughty boy'. His acting career involved usually playing a thug in programmes such as *London's Burning*, *Miss Marple* and *The Tomorrow People*. My favourite story involves Oprah Winfrey, a chippy in Gloucester and a delicious accompaniment. Tom used to frequent his local fish and chip shop in Matson in his youth and they did a fabulous curry sauce. He invented his own version and called it Matson Sauce, which can be found on his menu today. When dining in one of his restaurants, TV legend Oprah loved it so much she cornered Tom and asked him where it came from. He told her it was inspired by the estate he grew up on in Gloucestershire. She clearly got the wrong end of the stick as her follow-up questions revealed she assumed he grew up on his own country estate, clad in tweed, hosting shooting parties and making delicious sauces to go with the pike he had caught that morning in his private lake.

PUB NAMES EXPLAINED

I have often enjoyed a pint in the Basket Maker pub at Quedgeley. It was later known as the Weavers Arms, and now the Haywain. I never really thought too much about the name until I was told about a Mr Cale, who was a local basket weaver, and suddenly the penny dropped. It would be churlish not to visit some other favourite hostelries with classic tales behind them. I have always been intrigued and slightly amused when I see the sign for the Cock Inn at the start of the steep hill going out of Blakeney. In the days before motor vehicles, a cock was a big horse that could be hired to give extra pulling power on the hill. At busy times travellers waiting for the cock would buy refreshments from the house. The Mariners Arms in Berkeley is so called because boats used to sail up the Berkeley Pill and the mariners would walk to the pub. I would love to believe the next theory about one of Gloucester's best rugby pubs but I am not sure it is true. The Pelican, so it is claimed, was constructed out of timbers from Sir Francis Drake's ship *Golden Hind*, which was originally called the *Pelican*. The Glasshouse at May Hill is so named because of the Flemish glassmakers who settled there in the reign of Elizabeth I. Others with more obvious links include the Severn Bore at Minsterworth, the Anchor Inn at Epney, the Cheese Rollers at Shurdington, the Thames Head Inn near Kemble and, strike a light, I nearly forgot my local for thirty years, England's Glory, named after the matches produced in the nearby Moreland's match factory.

GREASY JOE'S, CIRENCESTER

My favourite ever roadside diner was a place called Greasy Joe's on the outskirts of Cirencester. It was a proper down-to-earth artery-hardening emporium of bacon, sausage and big steaming mugs of tea. It was also the place members of the SAS stopped on the way home after the Iranian embassy siege. From 30 April to 5 May 1980 the world watched as gunmen held twenty-six people hostage at the Iranian embassy in London. After a six-day stand-off, the SAS launched a dramatic attack on the hostage-takers. I interviewed one of the soldiers involved in the attack, Rusty Firmin, who told me that Greasy Joe's truckers' café in Cirencester was a regular stop-off for the SAS, and was visited by them just hours after the famous assault:

> From the 1970s we used to use that place. Travelling to and from London and back it was always a stop-off point either way. After the siege in the early hours of the morning, the vehicles were split up. Some would have left earlier than others, and I remember it was somewhere around three or four o'clock in the morning when we stopped off there. It was just a quick early morning breakfast but there was already another one of our vehicles there, so there ended up about six of us there in two vehicles. You could pull in on the side of the road … and buy whatever you wanted, from what was a big caravan type thing in those days. And I remember two sort of Billy Bunter guys behind the counter selling their wares – probably eating more than selling by the look of them but great guys and I remember them very well.

GLOUCESTER SERVICES

As a child heading up to Scotland on holiday, the one big treat was the inexplicable thrill of stopping off at the wonderful Tebay Services. There was nothing else quite like it. So, imagine my euphoria when we started reporting on a rumour that a similar enterprise might be coming to Gloucestershire. The driving force behind the project was an old friend of mine who I met in the 1990s when he was a community worker on the Matson estate in Gloucester. Mark Gale is one of life's gems. His mission was to create local, purposeful jobs for those living in the estates around Robinswood Hill. Conversations about how to utilise the nearby M5 for the local community began and the idea of a new motorway service station was born. The Gloucestershire Gateway Trust was duly formed and Mark went in search of a business partner.

'We went to find a business partner that held the same set of values as us, believed in locality, believed in local people and believed in local food. The Westmorland Family – they're the only local business that share the same set of values as us.'

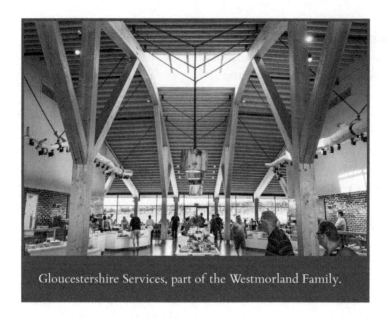

Gloucestershire Services, part of the Westmorland Family.

The Westmorland Family had created and run Tebay Services for many years and Mark knew this would be the perfect fit. The northbound services opened on 7 May 2014. The southbound services followed shortly after in May 2015, opened by the then Prince of Wales. The Gloucestershire Gateway Trust receives up to 3p in every £1 of non-fuel sales to invest in their local communities.

We are so proud of these services because of the ethos behind what they do and the reaction they receive from motorists from all over the UK. I once hosted my BBC breakfast show from the southbound side in peak tourist season to capture travellers on their way to Devon and Cornwall and persuade them to holiday in Gloucestershire the next summer. Many of us do our Christmas shopping here as the services are rammed with fantastic local products and I even once suggested to my wife, Jo, that the restaurant would be the perfect location to celebrate our twenty-fifth wedding anniversary.

How to Squeeze Every Drop Out of Glorious Gloucestershire's Gastronomy

Give your children/grandchildren the thrill of queuing up on Minchinhampton Common for a Winstones ice cream from the van, then go and fly a kite.

Save up and treat yourself at one of Cheltenham's award-winning fine dining restaurants.

Have lunch at the Thames Head pub, then find the source of the Thames (it's not far).

Scoff a Gloucester Dripper, readily available in local bakeries in the city.

Book your tickets early for the Frocester Beer Festival. It's brilliant but sells out quickly.

Take friends to lunch at the Glasshouse pub and show off your knowledge of its name's origin. Then, laden with local cheeses, head to the top of May Hill, look down on Dymock and raise a glass to Charles Martell while enjoying his Stinking Bishop.

Finally, call in at Gloucester Services, enjoy the farm shop and kitchen, revel in the ethos behind the company but maybe don't suggest it for a special romantic anniversary.

CUMMINGS' COUNTY QUIZ

ROUND TWO

1. True or false? Gloucestershire Police Force is one of the oldest in the country and was first formed to control lawlessness in the Forest of Dean.

2. Which famous singer-songwriter went to Wycliffe College in Stonehouse? Was it Donovan, who wrote 'Mellow Yellow'; Gordon Lightfoot, famous for the classic 'If You Could Read My Mind'; or Al Stewart, who penned the wonderful 'Year of the Cat'?

3. What is the derivation of the name Greet, a small village near Winchcombe: the gravelly place, the grey valley, or the settlement of the tobacco field?

4. It begins with an 's' and in their respective chaotic towns Stroud and Newent both have one.

5. Which of the following is not a market town: Stow-on-the-Wold, Moreton-in-Marsh or Bourton-on-the-Water?

6. Which of the following have never had a railway station: Bishop's Cleeve, Dymock or Tirley?

7. Is Quedgeley a town or a village?

8. What is Bob Dylan's link with the River Severn?

9. Which two Gloucestershire rivers have their source at Plynlimon in Wales?

10. Colonel Mad Jack Churchill was famous for what in 1955: being the first person to surf the Severn bore, the first person to run the 102-mile Cotswold Way in a day or the first person to abseil down the east window of Gloucester Cathedral?

3

SECRETS OF THE SEVERN

I WOULD LIKE to introduce you to a mysterious, mesmerising force in our county. Sabrina is the Latin name given to the River Severn and I intend to take you on a journey to squeeze every drop out of the UK's longest river. She bisects the county, providing a marker point for us all. She can delight us, calm us, feed us and kill us.

Sabrina is part of my soul because she is a constant presence and everywhere I go my heart swells when I catch glimpses of her. I have canoed across her, fished in her, waved at her from the top of the Severn Bridge and introduced numerous people to the magic of the Severn bore. You never forget your first bore. Mine was a night at Longney Crib with the legendary elver fisherman, Hartley Everett. It is such a thrill to see the reaction on people's faces when they first hear the thunderous sound of the bore approaching. River Severn expert Chris Witts has been my guest speaker at special bore-watching events for my radio show listeners. I have asked him to pen a few words on how to squeeze every drop out of the River Severn:

The River Severn enters the county as a young teenager, reaches the outskirts of the city of Gloucester and turns into a troublesome adolescent. Below Gloucester, as the river widens, it turns into a full-grown adult. Twice each month spring tides produce the famous Severn bore, a wave sweeping up the river from the estuary towards Gloucester. This is the largest bore in Europe, formed due to the Severn having the second highest rise and fall of tide in the world. At Minsterworth the river bank is often crowded by those wanting to watch this phenomenon, watching in awe as the large wave sweeps by.

Severn bore surfers. (Chris Witts)

The Purton Hulks.

Further down the Severn, on the opposite bank is Slimbridge Wetlands Centre, which today has the world's largest captive wildfowl collection. A favourite time to visit is on a cold, frosty winter's day to see the birds feeding. Travel a few miles further downriver and you will soon arrive at the village of Purton. Walking along the towpath of the Gloucester & Sharpness Canal, you will see the numerous barges that lie between the canal and the Severn foreshore. The canal is higher than the Severn and with exceptional high spring tides there's a chance the canal bank would be breached. This is why these old barges were beached here, now known as the Purton Hulks.

There are many more interesting places to visit along the Severn, including the port of Sharpness. Here, you can picnic alongside the piers to view ships close-up passing in and out of the port. Without doubt the River Severn is the most mighty of all rivers.

Afon Hafren is the Welsh name for the River Severn, harking back to a legendary princess who is said to live beneath its waters. These waters are dangerous, especially in the area called the Noose, below Arlingham, which is full of whirlpools, moving sandbanks and sinking sand. Gloucestershire is beyond proud and grateful to the Severn Area Rescue Association, a self-funded charity, who patrol the river and have saved countless lives.

I have been fortunate to view Sabrina from the top of the Severn Bridge. The ascent is fascinating. You go inside the big white stanchion and enter a tiny lift. At the end of a short rickety ride you exit still encased inside the top of the structure. There is a tiny ladder leading up to a porthole-style lid. Once out it is equally breathtaking and terrifying.

Beneath the bridge is a little island called Chapel Rock with an ancient ruined chapel that was originally dedicated to St Tecla. Locals used to bring food over for the hermit and the island is frequently cut off by dangerous tidal waters. When I filmed on this magical outcrop for BBC *Points West* we were glad it was the Severn Area Rescue team who had provided safe passage for us that day.

How to Squeeze Every Drop Out of the Severn

Visit the Purton Hulks. They are mysterious and awe inspiring. Look out across the river and see if you can spot the wrecks of the two tanker barges that collided in fog in 1960, prompting the Severn railway bridge disaster. The eerie remains of the *Wastdale* and the *Arkendale* can be seen at low tide.

Experience the Severn bore both in daylight and at night. The Severn Bore pub at Minsterworth is a good place to start. See the website seven-bore.co.uk for details.

My favourite vantage points for views of the Severn include the top of May Hill, where you really notice the acute bends around the Arlingham Horseshoe; on Rodborough Common towards the Prince Albert pub, where glancing a quick sliver warms the cockles; and Pleasant Style viewpoint just out of Littledean on the way to Newnham. I drive up and down Frocester Hill a lot and the view going down is sensational, although the temptation to peek while driving is potentially dangerous. My favourite close-up view is standing right at the end of Lydney Dock, where I feel a sense of peace and happy isolation.

A perfect view across the River Severn from Lydney Harbour.
(Forest of Dean and Wye Valley Tourism)

I always imagine that I could lean gently across the water and put my arms around Sharpness Docks and Berkeley Power Station and give them a great big cuddle. I have long arms.

Read more about the Severn on Chris Witts's severntales.co.uk website.

And finally let's end where we started, with Sabrina. You can listen to 'Sabrina – Goddess of the Severn' by local band Inkubus Sukkubus, which describes her as 'wild and free', or local folk legend Johnny Coppin's track 'Song of the Severn', which explores the legend of Sabrina:

Let your soul roll with the river
Deep in her water you'll be carried along.

4

GLOUCESTERSHIRE — THE ULTIMATE FILM SET

JOIN ME AS I transport you to the Gloucestershire streets, villages, houses and countryside that have been used as locations for some of the most famous films and TV shows ever made. Our journey will take us along wizard-festooned cloisters in Gloucester and to the Cheltenham park featured in a much-loved 1970s sitcom. We will hide from *Star Wars* villains among the trees in the Forest of Dean, call in at the Crossroads Motel from the long-running soap opera, chat to Pierce Brosnan in a Cotswold pub and catch up with various *Doctor Who* Doctors, who have popped up all over Glamorous Gloucestershire.

SNOWSHILL

This is the place to visit if you love a classic romcom, as Snowshill starred in *Bridget Jones's Diary*. The iconic scenes when Bridget visits her parents at Christmas were filmed across the parish, including on the village green, in the National Trust staff car park and at a house owned by the local Hooper family. Filming was carried out in July, so the whole village was covered in fake snow and flowers had to be cut off plants.

Snowshill, the location for the filming of *Bridget Jones*.

A40 GOLDEN VALLEY

In the early 1980s the opening shot of the motel in the TV soap opera *Crossroads* was filmed at the end of the Golden Valley, a stone's throw from where GCHQ is now. The Golden Valley Hotel could be seen every night opening the show for the much-loved and equally maligned soap opera that ran from the mid-1960s until 1988.

CHELTENHAM

There was an innocent magic about the Carla Lane late 1970s–early 1980s sitcom *Butterflies*, a TV show that was hugely popular and one many of us remember with great fondness. Starring Wendy Craig and Geoffrey Palmer, the series was set in Cheltenham and also starred a young Nicholas Lyndhurst as the younger son of Ria and Ben Parkinson. Ria was bored with her routine life and contemplated an affair with a dishy chap called Leonard. They used to meet secretly in a park and chat away on a bench near a lake, and the location used was Hatherley Park. The house where we often saw cars reversing on and off the drive was on

Bournside Road and many of the exteriors were shot in Montpellier and the High Street. My friend Patrick lives on Bournside Road and I asked him if he would mind me giving out his address and phone number so readers could book a *Butterflies* tour. Strangely he declined.

Cheltenham Town Hall featured in the TV adaptation of *Pride and Prejudice* and Cheltenham College was the location for the film *If* starring Malcolm McDowell.

BIBURY

It is a 50-mile round trip from my house in the south-west Cotswolds to Bibury and it had always been an ambition to cycle this route with my eldest daughter, Kate. It was partly a physical challenge but there was also the allure of Arlington Row and what that signified. When Kate was young we made a tradition of going to Cheltenham at Christmas

Dad and daughter cycling pilgrimage
to Arlington Row, Bibury.

and always went to the cinema. One year we saw the film *Stardust* with Sienna Miller and Claire Danes and it was an unforgettable dad and daughter experience. Arlington Row in Bibury features in the film, so it was a special pilgrimage for us both and involved the obligatory photograph. It is a much-photographed street with its stone cottages, which were built in 1380 as a monastic wool store and converted into a row of weavers' cottages in the seventeenth century.

The National Trust owns the Arlington Row cottages and leases them out to private tenants. One of these tenants once told me they were having a bed delivered one morning and she opened the door for the two chaps to carry her new furniture inside. As they entered her house along came three Japanese tourists behind them who promptly sat down in her lounge, assuming it was some sort of tourist attraction.

BOURTON-ON-THE-WATER

In 2002 I received a phone call from a very happy pub landlord at the Old Manse pub in Bourton-on-the-Water. He shared the story of Pierce Brosnan and some of the other crew popping in for a drink during filming of the latest Bond film. Apparently, he was a lovely man who signed autographs for anyone who asked. He was spending his time zipping around car parks in Bourton-on-the-Water and the former RAF runway at nearby Little Rissington for the ice car chase sequences in *Die Another Day*.

NORTHLEACH

If you want to find the filming locations for the BAFTA-winning *This Country*, head to Northleach. Siblings Daisy May and Charlie Cooper devised and wrote the series, which was influenced by their life growing up around Cirencester. If you check out 'A Mucklowe Funeral' in series three, see if you can spot their real-life Northleach neighbour, rock legend Steve Winwood, outside the pub.

GLOUCESTER CATHEDRAL

Gloucester Cathedral appeared in three of the Harry Potter films: *Harry Potter and the Philosopher's Stone*, *Harry Potter and the Chamber of Secrets* and *Harry Potter and the Half-Blood Prince*. The buzz around the city when the stars arrived and the movie sets were constructed was a thing to behold. It was always fun wandering around the cathedral at lunchtime chatting up the security team and watching the fans try to sneak through the barricades. The filming took place in the magical cloisters, so have a good look around and see if you can find the following scenes. The north part of the cloisters is referred to as the Lavatorium, the washing place, and it was the perfect hiding place for Harry and Ron in the first film. Head to the south side and you will find yourself in the hallway where all the first-year Gryffindors walk on their first visit to the Common Room. On the north side try to spot the place where the message 'the Chamber of Secrets has been opened' appears in the second film. Finally, on the east corridor imagine the hallway in the scene where the girls' bathroom was flooded, supposedly by Moaning Myrtle, in *Chamber of Secrets*.

Gloucestershire Cathedral's cloisters,
where *Harry Potter* was filmed.

The cathedral has also been used to film *Doctor Who*. Jodie Whittaker came for the filming of *Fugitive of the Judoon*. She apparently charmed everyone she met on set. Among the many other classics filmed here were *Sherlock* starring Benedict Cumberbatch; Hilary Mantel's *Wolf Hall* with Claire Foy, Damian Lewis and Mark Rylance; and *Mary Queen of Scots*, featuring Saoirse Ronan and Margot Robbie.

PUZZLEWOOD

Doctor Who has a habit of popping up all over the county. The eleventh Doctor, Matt Smith, filmed both his first and final episodes at Puzzlewood. Peter Capaldi took over from him in the 2013 Christmas special *The Time of the Doctor*, filmed here. This magical, ancient wood near Coleford is a movie director's dream, summed up by Kathleen Kennedy, *Star Wars* producer and president of Lucasfilm, as 'the most magical forest on the face of the earth! I've spoken to Star Wars fans from around the globe who have made a pilgrimage.' *Star Wars: Episode VII: The Force Awakens* was filmed at Puzzlewood.

The magical, mysterious Puzzlewood. (Forest of Dean and Wye Valley Tourism)

Other big productions include *Jack the Giant Slayer*, starring Ewan McGregor and Stanley Tucci. All five series of *Merlin* were filmed at Puzzlewood, a perfect backdrop for the ancient world of Albion and creatures such as unicorns and dragons. The wood also made the ideal setting for *The Secret Garden*, starring Colin Firth and Julie Walters. Finally, our fabulous forest featured in the opening titles of an episode of *Our Planet* narrated by Sir David Attenborough, highlighting the fragile interdependence between all the creatures that live in the forest environment.

CLEARWELL CAVES

Super fans of *Doctor Who* have another location to add to their time travel map of glittering Gloucestershire. These caves were visited four times by the Doctor with parts of episodes including *The Christmas Invasion*; *The Satan Pit*; *The Time of Angels*; and *Flesh and Stone* all filmed there.

WYE VALLEY

Netflix's hugely popular *Sex Education* is another example of why the Forest of Dean and surrounding areas are such a popular choice. The following locations all feature: Bathurst Pool in Lydney; Dean Forest Railway's Parkend station; Redbrook's bridge; and St Briavels Castle. The red and white house, known as The Chalet, is perched in woodland at Symonds Yat.

GLOUCESTER DOCKS

This waterside location has provided work for both Captain Birdseye and Johnny Depp. Disney came here to film the sequel to Tim Burton's *Alice in Wonderland*. The production of *Alice Through the Looking Glass*, starring Johnny Depp as the Mad Hatter, took over Gloucester Docks for a week. Filming involved 300 crew, 150 extras, five tall ships, eighteen horses and a couple of llamas. The docks were also used for one of the Captain Birdseye fishfinger adverts and the 1970s Sunday evening drama *The Onedin Line*, starring Peter Gilmore as James Onedin.

Captain Birdseye advert filmed at Gloucester Docks. (Chris Witts)

CHAVENAGE HOUSE

This Elizabethan house has been used for many productions, including *Lark Rise to Candleford*, *Cider with Rosie*, Agatha Christie's *The Pale Horse*, *Tess of the d'Urbervilles* and *Wolf Hall*. It is best known, however, as the setting for Trenwith in *Poldark*. Chavenage just happens to be on one of my regular cycle routes and whenever they were filming *Poldark*, the lane past the house was often cordoned off from middle-aged Lycra louts like me. Every time this happened we would ask security if the producers needed a body double to give Aidan Turner a break. We would start peeling off our sweaty cycling tops for extra comedy effect, to the utter derision and bemusement of the head of security. You can't put a price on comedy. Other *Poldark* scenes were filmed at the nearby Royal Agricultural University at Cirencester.

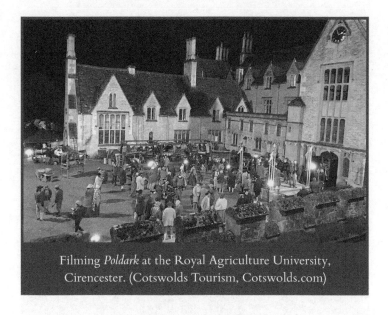

Filming *Poldark* at the Royal Agriculture University, Cirencester. (Cotswolds Tourism, Cotswolds.com)

SAPPERTON AND MISERDEN

There have been many screen adaptations of Laurie Lee's *Cider with Rosie* but most were not filmed in Slad where the book is set. Miserden has been a popular location, with the Carpenters Arms pub doubling up as the Woolpack. In 1998 the village of Sapperton was used for exterior shots and after filming had wrapped up one local phoned my radio show to tell me the production crew had left a bottle of champagne on everyone's doorstep as a thank you for putting up with the filming.

OLDBURY

This decommissioned power station is in South Gloucestershire but I love the stories so much, I am including it. In *The Hand of Fear* from the 1970s, Tom Baker as the Doctor spent some time on top of the power station. *Top of the Pops* also filmed Slade stomping about singing along to 'Gudbuy T'Jane'. According to my sources, it took a day to film while the plant was operating. They filmed on the floor above the reactor and on a trolley up and down a corridor. Oldbury has hosted the stars of *Blake's 7*, episodes of *Tomorrow's World* and even the National Monopoly Championship.

Mark Williams as *Father Brown* on location near Moreton.
(Cotswolds Tourism, Cotswolds.com)

BLOCKLEY

This is the location for the long-running popular drama *Father Brown*, based on the stories by G.K. Chesterton. Featuring a fictional crime-solving Roman Catholic priest in the 1950s played by actor Mark Williams, it shows off the Cotswolds to their finest. Other locations used in the series include Guiting Power, Sudeley Castle, Moreton Hospital, Winchcombe and Upper Slaughter.

BERKELEY CASTLE

This is a magnificent castle to visit, run by a brilliant team who take great care in sharing the history and bringing the past back to life. It is another Gloucestershire location used as a setting for *Poldark* and *Wolf Hall*, as well as *The Other Boleyn Girl* and the children's series *The Ghost Hunter*. With a bit of smoke and mirrors, the castle was made to look as if it was on an island in the middle of the ocean as the setting for the G8 summit in *Johnny English Strikes Again*.

STANWAY HOUSE

This beautiful Jacobean manor house near Winchcombe was yet another place used for *Wolf Hall*, as well as the TV series *Jeeves and Wooster*, *Vanity Fair* and *The Libertine*, starring Johnny Depp.

SWINHAY HOUSE

The first time I caught sight of this building I was walking in the hills above Wotton-under-Edge and thought I was hallucinating. The imposing, futuristic mansion Swinhay House featured as a criminal mastermind's lair in *Sherlock*. It is owned by Sir David McMurtry, the boss of the local engineering firm Renishaw. I have friends who work for his company who have told me how mind-blowing it was to have their Christmas party in that very house.

Futuristic Swinhay House, where *Sherlock* was filmed.

WOODCHESTER MANSION

I went for a walk into the Woodchester Valley the day after I had binge watched far too many episodes of *The Crown*. As Woodchester Mansion appeared in the valley below, I was transported back into the Netflix drama and I thought I might well bump into Prince Philip or Prince Charles. The previous evening, I had watched the episode that featured their differing experiences of Gordonstoun School in Scotland. The mansion provided the setting not just for the school's exterior but also the nearby lakes and boathouse were heavily featured, too. Other films and TV shows filmed here include *His Dark Materials* and *The Famous Five*.

How to Squeeze Every Drop Out of Glorious Gogglebox Gloucestershire

Re-watch the Harry Potter films, then head off to Gloucester Cathedral cloisters; buy a lightsabre and get lost in Puzzlewood.

Book a Woodchester Mansion ghost hunting experience.

Enjoy the wonderful re-enactment days at Berkeley Castle, and then take a walk high up above Wotton-under-Edge and try to spot the mind-blowing Swinhay House below.

The following are things you must not do: strip off in front of a security guard pretending to be Poldark at Chavenage; walk into someone's front room on Arlington Row; and definitely don't get caught holding hands with a mystery companion on a bench in Hatherley Park.

CUMMINGS' COUNTY QUIZ

ROUND THREE

1. True or false? In the 1980s, Gloucester rugby stars Ben Miller and Jerry Gardner conducted a celebrity opening of an extension to Wall's social club. The witty headline in the following day's *Citizen* newspaper was 'Wall's Ice Cream get help from Ben and Jerry'.

2. Where would you find the Wishing Clock?

3. What business is Jessie Smith known for?

4. Chipping Campden and Chipping Norton – which one is in Gloucestershire?

5. The Reverend Wilbert Awdry retired to Rodborough but what is he famous for?

6. A cat called Simpkin features in which famous Gloucestershire work of literature?

7. In which year did Gifford's Circus start: 1997, 2000 or 2005?

8. Did Longlevens once have a large outdoor swimming pool, croquet lawns or a greyhound track?

9. The famous A40 runs right through the county but where in the west does it end its journey?

10. What did William the Conqueror order while in Gloucester in 1085?

5

IN THE FOOTSTEPS
OF DICK WHITTINGTON

JUST IN CASE anyone is in any doubt, Dick Whittington was real, he did walk to London and the fortune he made there is still being used today for good causes. I think that is what you call a legacy. There was only one way to share this spectacular story with the world. I had to walk the walk. In 2005 the city of Gloucester was preparing to commemorate the 400th anniversary of the first play about Dick Whittington and as part of those celebrations the BBC commissioned a radio drama narrative entitled *The Hitherto Unrecorded Memoirs of Richard Whittington, Mercer*. Additionally, some unwitting breakfast show radio presenter was duped into walking from Whittington's birthplace in Gloucestershire all the way to London.

Dick Whittington setting
off from Gloucester.

Dick Whittington leaves Cirencester on his way to London.

The idea was to dispel the notion that he was just a pantomime character swaggering along with his sandwiches wrapped in a red spotted handkerchief on the end of a stick. On Saturday, 28 May 2005 I led a bunch of passionate storytellers on a walk of a lifetime.

This was our route:

Saturday, 28 May: Pauntley Court, Newent to Cirencester
Sunday, 29 May: Cirencester to Lechlade
Monday, 30 May: Lechlade to Wantage
Tuesday, 31 May: Wantage to Ridgeway on horseback and Goring to Caversham
Wednesday, 1 June: Caversham to Henley-on-Thames, then to Maidenhead via the Thames Path
Thursday, 2 June: Maidenhead to Richmond by boat aboard the river cruiser *Fringilla*
Friday, 3 June: Richmond to Barnes Bridge via the Thames Path, and Hampstead to Highgate
Saturday, 4 June: Highgate Hill and a visit to the Whittington Hospital, then to the City of London for a reception in the Mansion House with the Lord Mayor of London

Along the way we deepened our knowledge about the man and his life. We told stories of his childhood growing up at Pauntley Court near Newent with his wealthy family. We explored what his journey to London would have been like. Our research suggested some of it would have been done on horseback. Accommodation along the route would have been basic and bawdy. The hostelries would have been full of dubious characters. For historical accuracy we stayed in similar places and it was later noted that the dubious characters we encountered were each other. When Whittington arrived in London he was employed as a merchant by Sir William Warren, a mercer and a relative of Dick's. Dick learned about the delights of mercery and was given a stark choice. 'The choice is yours ... It's the stench of the city or the sight and satisfaction of the silk purse. Which will it be?'

He had a swift and successful progression up the ranks as a member of the Company of Mercers and made a lot of money. He had influential friends, among them King Richard II. It was Richard who first appointed him Mayor of London.

Life wasn't all plain sailing, however. Just when he seemed to be at the peak of success and authority, the tide of fortune turned. Richard II was deposed and Dick's wife Alice died. The pain of her death never left him.

He was chosen by his colleagues to be Mayor of London three more times. Among his memories was the banquet in honour of Henry V's victory at Agincourt. An early clue to his compassion was his ban on washing animal skins in the Thames. This ended a practice that saw many young boys dying of hyperthermia while carrying out the task.

Whittington's financial legacy was immense. He was a widower for many years and, being childless, he insisted his wealth should be devoted to the poor and destitute. He earned the title of 'the model merchant of the Middle Ages'.

We wanted to let everyone know of his altruism and what he did when he was alive but also to highlight how his life's work is still helping people. Money he left paid for Whittington College, thirteen almshouses and the restoration of St Bartholomew's Hospital in Smithfield. Six hundred years after his death, the Charity of Sir Richard Whittington pays out huge amounts for needy causes. In 1948 an amalgamation of several hospitals was named the Whittington Hospital, and other funds more recently have been used to help and protect women who have been sex-trafficked from Eastern Europe. New accommodation in East Grinstead has been funded and has provided homes for elderly women.

It was a privilege to walk the walk and talk the talk. Gloucestershire should be so proud of this man and I hope by retelling the true story of his life and legacy more people can see the magic behind the myth.

CUMMINGS' COUNTY QUIZ

ROUND FOUR

1. True or false? In 1987 Keith Harris and Orville were booked to open a new viewing area at the Wildfowl and Wetlands Centre at Slimbridge. When senior management found out, they considered this PR stunt to be inappropriate and risked diminishing Sir Peter Scott's legacy. The booking was cancelled but Harris was still paid his £2,000 fee. Orville was said to be philosophical about the whole affair.

2. If you went from Toddington to Broadway by train, which railway company would you be using?

3. How did Cavendish House in Cheltenham, which recently closed down, get its name: after Sir William Cavendish, the town's MP, after a race horse called Cavendish Boy, or after Cavendish Square in London where the original owner started their career?

4. Which Gloucester school did Sir Robin Day go to?

5. Which is higher, Littledean or Cinderford?

6. According to legend, how many trees are there in Painswick churchyard? It is believed the devil will not allow an extra tree to grow to reach a certain round number.

7. What is Innsworth Barracks now known as?

8. Which opened first, Gloucester Services Northbound or Southbound?

9. What did Robert Holford plant: a new grass pitch at Kingsholm, snowdrops at Painswick Rococo Gardens or the first trees at Westonbirt Arboretum?

10. Somerford Keynes and Ashton Keynes are close to each other along the Spine Road that separates Gloucestershire and Wiltshire. Which of them is in Gloucestershire?

6

LEAVING A LEGACY

INVENTIONS, COMPANIES AND PEOPLE WHO HAVE CHANGED THE WORLD

IN THIS CHAPTER I would like to stretch the definition of the word 'legacy' into areas that might surprise you. We will show off the way Gloucestershire people and businesses have changed the world, how our landscape and architecture have been a lasting inspiration and meet local legends who have been responsible for many words and phrases we use in daily life.

1. INVENTIONS

My heart bursts with pride when I think about all this county's inventions. From life-saving cures to powered flight, instant custard to the lawnmower, we have done it all. Famous Gloucestershire folk have had a profound impact on the environment, theology and technology that has left a living legacy for future generations. Let's enjoy what this amazing county has inspired and look forward to the future by celebrating the exciting innovation happening right now.

Statue of Edward Jenner at
Gloucester Cathedral.

Cure for Smallpox

Edward Jenner was born in Berkeley on 17 May 1749 and he invented the smallpox vaccination. One of the most important jobs I had as a broadcaster during the coronavirus pandemic was to share vital, potentially life-saving information with my audience. Announcing the help that was available at the Edward Jenner Unit at the Gloucestershire Royal Hospital always made my heart race a little faster. The fact that you could get your COVID vaccine here, at the place named after the man synonymous with the word vaccine, was a true thrill. In 1796, he carried out his now famous experiment on 8-year-old James Phipps. He inserted pus taken from a cowpox pustule into an incision on the boy's arm. The theory came from local folklore that milkmaids who caught the mild disease of cowpox never contracted smallpox. He subsequently proved that, having been inoculated with cowpox, Phipps was immune to smallpox. He experimented on several other children, including his own 11-month-old son. In 1798, the results were finally published and Jenner coined the word vaccination from the Latin *vacca* for cow.

Jet Engine

Sir Frank Whittle was born on 1 June 1907 and his jet engine was designed and built in Gloucestershire. When you wander through the Regent Arcade in Cheltenham you are stepping over the hallowed ground that used to be the garage and the workshop of 'the man who shrunk the world'. It was here at the Regent Garage where Whittle invented the jet engine. In 2002 the BBC tasked each radio station in the west to nominate a local hero and compete to have a documentary made about them. I chose Whittle and we beat off competition from Bristol, Wiltshire and Somerset to become the clear winner of the BBC's Local Heroes poll. The programme told the story of the first jet flight at Brockworth, Gloucester, in May 1941 when test pilot Gerry Sayer lifted the Gloster E.28/39 aircraft off the runway.

The Whittle programme revealed that despite claims that RAF Cranwell was the location of the ground-breaking event, Sir Frank himself considered the Brockworth test to be the first flight of an aircraft powered by his jet engine.

To mark the television broadcast, I hosted the screening of a documentary to an audience of 200 at the University of Gloucester in Oxtalls, which we entitled *Frank Whittle: The Man Who Shrank the World*.

Gloster E.28/39 replica at the Jet Age Museum. (David Hanks)

The guest of honour was Ian Whittle, Sir Frank's son. He flew from the south coast especially for the event and was delighted by the response. Ian said:

> This is where it all started as far as jet flight is concerned in this country. The people here have every right to feel proud and I, myself, feel proud of my father. I was amazed that in the West Country people remembered him. I thought you'd all forgotten about him here. I'm very pleased and very honoured on behalf of my father.

It was such a thrill to host the event and meet Ian as well as those who worked on the aircraft.

Lawnmower

Edwin Beard Budding was born in Eastington, a few miles west of Stroud, on 25 August 1796 and he invented both the lawnmower and the adjustable spanner. The inspiration for the lawnmower came from seeing a cross-cutting machine used to finish woollen cloth in a local Stroud mill. There is a blue plaque dedicated to him at Stroud Brewery, located

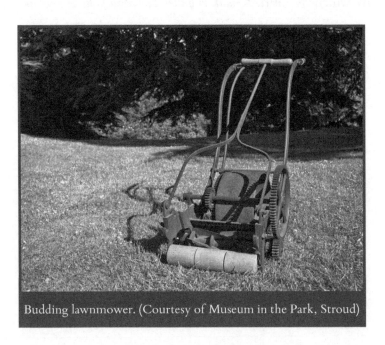

Budding lawnmower. (Courtesy of Museum in the Park, Stroud)

in Thrupp on the site of the factory where Budding made mowers with local engineer John Ferrabee. Today, Stroud Brewery produces its very own Budding Pale Ale to mark their connection to the famous inventor. Examples of the early Budding mowers can be seen at Stroud Museum in the Park.

Shorthand
Sir Isaac Pitman was born on 4 January 1813 in Wiltshire and he came up with the notion of shorthand while teaching in Wotton-under-Edge. He taught first at the British School and later set up his own. He invented his 'phonography' or shorthand in 1837 while living in Orchard Street, where the Grade II listed Pitman House still stands complete with commemorative blue plaque.

Horlicks
William Horlick was born on 23 February 1846 in Ruardean in the Forest of Dean and he invented the popular malted milk drink Horlicks with his brother James. If you take a peek behind the Malt Shovel pub you can still see the shed where some say this milky/malty night-time comfort drink was dreamt up which went on to become a global favourite.

Ribena
The Forest of Dean can claim another famous drink in the inventions list: Ribena. Dr Vernon Charley was a leading scientist at the University of Bristol and lived for most of his life in the Forest of Dean. He came up with the recipe for a blackcurrant syrup in 1938 after noticing that blackcurrants contained high levels of vitamin C. Ribena was given to children and expectant mothers for free during the Second World War when other fruits with vitamin C were hard to acquire. Ribena is still made to this day at the factory in Coleford in the Forest of Dean.

Vacuum Cleaner
Hubert Cecil Booth was born on 4 July 1871 in Gloucester and he invented the vacuum cleaner. The eureka moment happened when he saw a demonstration of a new carpet-cleaning machine for railway carriages at St Pancras Station. The machine used a method of blowing air into a dust box using high-pressure jets. Booth decided a far better

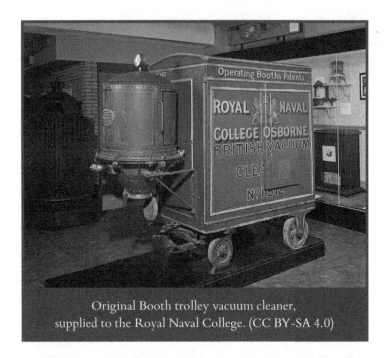

Original Booth trolley vacuum cleaner,
supplied to the Royal Naval College. (CC BY-SA 4.0)

method would be to use suction, so our Gloucester boy cracked it by going home and developing a vacuum cleaner driven by a piston engine. The first cleaner didn't come cheap as it cost about £350. A perfect advert fell into his lap when he was invited to clean the carpet at Westminster Abbey just before the coronation of Edward VII, and vacuum cleaning units were installed at both Buckingham Palace and Windsor Castle for a royal clean sweep. Booth was a prolific innovator and he also invented the Ferris wheel and designed engines for battleships. There is a blue plaque on Park House in Montpellier area of Gloucester where he lived.

Instant Custard
God bless Alfred Bird, who was born in 1811 in Nympsfield and came up with the notion of instant custard because his wife was allergic to egg. Bird's Custard was first formulated and cooked in 1837, and the story goes that at a dinner party, the Booths served their guests not the egg-based custard as they had intended but rather the instant egg-free variety by mistake. The dessert was gobbled up with great appreciation, which inspired Alfred Bird to put the recipe into wider production.

Badminton

We didn't invent the sport of badminton but a place in the county (now South Gloucestershire) was the inspiration for the name we now know it by. The beginnings of the sport can be traced to the mid-1800s, when it was created by British military officers stationed in British India. Originally called 'battledore and shuttlecock', players would try to hit the shuttlecock as many times as possible without it hitting the ground. In the late 1800s, the game was brought back to this country by retired army officers and played at the Duke of Beaufort's home, Badminton House in Gloucestershire. From that point onwards, the game became known as badminton.

Pederson Bicycle

I have met fellow cyclists who own a Pederson bike and I am convinced it's the love of their life. If you 'get it' there is no finer way to explore Gloucestershire on two wheels. It was developed by the Danish inventor Mikael Pederson and produced in his adopted home of Dursley. The bike has an unusual frame with a hammock-style saddle. Pederson is loved in the town and I found it very moving to see his wonderful gravestone in the local cemetery with an image of the bike and the words 'The Last Journey'. I subsequently learned when chatting to locals that in 1995, following a campaign and collection for funds, Mikael Pedersen's remains were exhumed from their unmarked grave in Denmark and re-interred in Dursley cemetery.

The Electric Telegraph, English Concertina and So Much More

Sir Charles Wheatstone was born in 1802 in Barnwood, Gloucester, and as well as a brilliant mind, he has a staggering CV of inventiveness. I am not sure we celebrate this man enough, so I am pleased to include some of his greatest achievements here. He developed the Wheatstone bridge, which is used to measure an unknown electrical resistance and made possible the first commercial electric telegraph. This early incarnation of communications technology means we can safely say he is one of the minds behind the digitally connected world we live in today. Wheatstone also invented the concertina and introduced stereo photography, for which he is regarded as 'the father of 3D and virtual reality technology'.

Fortified Steel

Where would we have been without fortified steel? Robert Forester Mushet was born in 1811 in Coleford in the Forest of Dean and he invented a type of steel that was stronger than the steel of the day. He was such an enthusiast, he and his father set up a metallurgical research laboratory in their garden. In the first years of railways, a rail's life expectancy was short-lived but Mushet developed more durable high-quality steel, meaning that less maintenance was needed. He took over the management of his father's ironworks at Darkhill near Coleford and his rails lasted for a good ten years compared to the previous lifetime of a few months.

Chicken in a Basket

My listeners have told me they used to love going to the Mill pub in Withington in the Cotswolds back in the 1960s, where it is claimed the concept of chicken in a basket was invented. Who am I to argue?

2. GLOUCESTERSHIRE PEOPLE WHO HAVE LEFT THEIR MARK ON THE WORLD

George Holloway

There is one local legend who was way ahead of his time. His legacy stands firm today and his inspirational story led to the making of my proudest 'moment' on the radio. George Holloway's impact on Stroud and the wider world revolved around his innovation and altruism. He set up the Holloway Clothing Factory in 1849 and it was famous worldwide for many innovations. It claimed to be the first to use steam for the manufacture of clothes, and the first to produce off-the-peg clothes (previously, items would have been made to measure by a tailor). George Holloway thought of himself as a philanthropist. His theory was that if you looked after your workers, their loyalty and hard work would reap rich rewards. He was the first to introduce a system of sick pay and a lump sum payment at retirement way before any notion of a benefits system. This was the beginning of the Holloway Friendly Society, which is still going today. The company also introduced the first rent-to-buy scheme, acquiring over seventy cottages in Stroud and renting them to workers. If workers paid a little extra than the going rate they could eventually own their home. If that wasn't enough, George was also the town's MP from 1886 to 1892.

This radio 'moment' I referred to earlier started with my love of the hooters, whistles and sirens that used to resound across Gloucestershire from Lister Petter in Dursley, to the Gloster Aircraft Company in Brockworth and Northern United near Cinderford. The Holloway Clothing Company had a steam whistle that one of my listeners, Faye Woodward, just happened to have on her mantelpiece. Her father worked at the factory and was given the whistle as a leaving present. Her abiding memory of her father was the daily routine of joining him at the factory every evening and her treat was to sound the whistle to announce the end of the working day. She called my show, told me the story and I decided we needed to get it blasting out across the valleys again. With the help of the team at the engineering company Spirax Sarco and their steam propulsion expertise, we got it going again at their base in Cheltenham. Now it was time to bring it back to the site of the factory in Stroud and wake up the Five Valleys again.

The sub-plot to our noisy adventure was the wonderful stories and characters we unearthed in the making of the show. The best bit by far was meeting many of the workers, who all seemed proud to have been associated with Holloways. I recreated the 1950s bus journey into work from Chalford with Margaret and Shelia, who were just 15 at the time. They behaved very badly on my coach, with deeply indiscreet stories about the bosses they didn't like, the boys they fancied and the lunchtimes they spent eating chips in Stroud when they should have gone to the work's canteen. I also met Iris and Peter, who met at the bus stop outside the Sub Rooms and were celebrating their sixtieth wedding anniversary.

And so it came to pass, bringing the Holloway whistle back to Stroud. This moment had been in the planning for months, and one morning just before 8 a.m. on the former site of the company at Brick Row in Stroud we gathered a steam engine, the actual whistle, the owner of the whistle, a cast of former workers and TV crews. People were also positioned around the Stroud valleys to monitor how far away it could be heard and a nervous radio host was wondering what could possibly go wrong? Thankfully nothing. It was heard as far away as Edge, Painswick, Eastington, Whiteshill and Rodborough, and the memories

Faye Woodward bringing her father's
Holloway whistle back to life.

and emotions it brought back flooded the airwaves. People called me in tears because it reminded them of a time and place in their lives, either walking to school, heading off to work or the relief of hearing the whistle in the evening marking the end of the working day. It all started with Faye and her dad, and to see the look on her face when she heard the whistle sound again in the exact spot she used to go every evening with her late father made all the work, worry and stress worthwhile. Thank you, Mr Holloway, for the thousands of jobs you provided, the impact of your social reform and for turning me into an official whistle-blower.

Sir Peter Scott

Sir David Attenborough described Sir Peter Scott as 'The Patron Saint of Conservation'. He said, 'Peter Scott was a huge influence on my childhood … later on in life I had the good fortune both to meet and interview him and he remains, for me, a hero.' He was talking about the man who set up the Wildfowl and Wetlands Trust at Slimbridge in 1946. There are now ten WWT wetland reserves with 1,000 volunteers, 450 staff, 200,000 members and 1 million visitors a year, of which 50,000 are schoolchildren learning about the environment.

Broadcasting live from Sir Peter Scott's lounge at Slimbridge.

One of my favourite outside broadcasts was from Sir Peter's iconic lounge when this special room became available for the public to view. The room, which he referred to as his studio lounge, was the site of the BBC's first ever live natural history programme in May 1953. So why is the house so important? It was within these walls that the global system for designating species as threatened, endangered or extinct was devised. To spend a few hours broadcasting in this environment was a privilege but don't take my word for it, what does the governor have to say? Sir David Attenborough was inspired hugely by Scott's early TV work and commented:

Long before words like 'biodiversity' were coined, Peter looked out from that huge window in his house at Slimbridge and realised our lives are so linked with our natural world that we have to learn to look after it. I think it's wonderful that absolutely anyone will be able to sit in that same window in future years and feel just as inspired.

George Whitfield

How do you sum up this man's influence across the world? One of the founders of Methodism, he has been described as the most influential Anglo-American evangelical preacher and 'the most famous man in the world' in the eighteenth century. He was born in Gloucester in 1714 at the Bell Inn on Southgate Street, educated at the Crypt School and gave his first sermon at St Mary de Crypt Church. He is estimated to have preached at least 18,000 times during his lifetime to millions of people.

Robert Raikes

George Whitfield had a huge influence on another Gloucester-born 'influencer'. Robert Raikes was born in Gloucester in 1736 and is best known for founding the Sunday School movement as well as being passionate about prison reform. His father owned the influential *Gloucester Journal* and Robert attended the St Mary de Crypt Grammar School. Growing up, he was aware of Whitfield's ministry and the Wesley brothers were regular visitors to the Raikes's family home.

Robert Raikes's House, Gloucester.

Although Sunday schools already existed, it was Raikes who really accelerated the movement in Britain. Poverty at the time meant that children were forced to work long hours every day except Sundays to support their families. This left little time for learning, so Raikes launched a school on Sundays in Southgate Street with an emphasis on literacy, although the Bible was used as a textbook. Behaviour in the city improved and Raikes took the opportunity to promote the success of the Sunday schools popping up elsewhere in Gloucester in the *Gloucester Journal*. John Wesley was a family friend, and thanks to his endorsement news of the Sunday school success spread nationwide.

Raikes's concern for prison reform was prompted by a visit to Gloucester Jail, where he witnessed the conditions inmates were enduring. After inheriting and taking over his father's newspaper, he was able to make regular appeals for food, clothing and small amounts of money for the prisoners.

The house on Southgate Street where Raikes lived and worked is now a pub called Robert Raikes's House and is a constant reminder of the huge influence he had on the Sunday School movement.

William Tyndale

I always get a warm glow when I see the towering Tyndale Monument on the Cotswold Escarpment above North Nibley. You can see it from Lydney Docks, the M5 or, my personal favourite, on the Whiteway Hill dropping down into Dursley. The monument is 111 ft tall and was built in honour of William Tyndale, who was born nearby at Stinchcombe in approximately 1494. Tyndale translated the Bible from Orthodox Greek into English, which was controversial and risky at the time but he was determined that everyone should have access to the scriptures.

I made a film about Tyndale for the BBC and what struck me most was the love and pride the people of North Nibley have for him. I was filming at the top of the monument when I saw a farmer ploughing deep down in the valley below and I knew this was the perfect image to sum up Tyndale's mission because he believed every ploughboy in the land should have the chance to read the Bible. Sadly, he was eventually condemned for heresy and executed by strangulation, with his body burned at the stake.

Frederick Sanger

Frederick Sanger was born in 1918 at Rendcomb near Cirencester. He was a biochemist who was twice awarded the Nobel Prize for Chemistry. He was awarded the prize in 1958 for his work on the structure of the insulin molecule and again in 1980 for his work in DNA sequencing methods.

Joe Henson

What a thrill it was to meet this kind, innovative and visionary man. The late Joe Henson left the most amazing legacy with his passion for championing rare breeds in the 1960s and '70s before it was fashionable. His work encouraged a thriving national movement to form and helped to save famous varieties of farm animals that might otherwise have vanished.

The Cotswold Park Farm was originally set up in 1971 and some of us remember it as a much smaller operation with an array of unusual breeds of pigs, sheep, goats, cattle, horses, ponies and poultry spread around the land in no particular order. It was low key, welcoming and helped educate generations of visiting families and schoolchildren about the importance of breeding pedigree livestock and maintaining diversity

Joe Henson in his element with a Golden Guernsey.

among farm animals. Joe founded the Rare Breeds Survival Trust in 1973. His amazing legacy continues today with the much-expanded Cotswold Farm Park, often featured on the BBC programme *Countryfile* with Joe's son, Adam, who along with the rest of the family is keeping Joe's vision alive.

Charles Martell

I love chatting to this man because he is an intriguing mixture of bluntness, infectious energy, innovation and he doesn't suffer fools. All of these attributes tell of a man who has made a huge impact in our county that will last for generations. People know of him as the cheesemaker who gave us Stinking Bishop cheese so loved by Wallace and Gromit but there is a lot more to him than this. Like Joe Henson, Charles is passionate about local provenance and has kept a herd of more than twenty Gloucester cattle at his farm in Dymock since 1972, producing cheeses such as Single Gloucester, which is backed with Protection of Designated Origin (PDO) status. He believes in protecting the county breed and providing what visitors and customers expect, Gloucester cheese and Gloucester beef. As I write I have in front of me a prized possession, *Native Apples of Gloucestershire* by Charles Martell. This book is a definitive account of almost 200 indigenous varieties of Gloucestershire apples. Charles has rediscovered and propagated 106 of these varieties, which now form the National Collection of Gloucestershire Apples and are planted on his Dymock farm. He is one of Gloucestershire's many food heroes.

3. COMPANIES THAT HAVE CHANGED THE WORLD

H.H. Martyn & Co. Ltd

When I speak to anyone who has links with this incredible company the pride oozes out of them, and for very good reason. This firm cemented the county's role in aerospace technology history by giving us the Gloster Aircraft Company and a link to another local firm, Dowty. Among some of the famous items produced by the company are the iron gates at Marble Arch, decorative interior work at Buckingham Palace and Windsor Castle and interiors of ships including *Titanic* and *QE2*. They are even responsible for the Speaker's Chair and dispatch boxes in the House of Commons.

The company was established by Herbert Henry Martyn in 1888 in Cheltenham on the corner of College Road and the High Street. It began as a firm of stone, marble and wood carvers who made gravestones and memorials before moving into joinery, decorative plaster work and wrought iron work. The Gloster Aircraft Company was formed after Martyn's were sub-contracted to make military planes. One of their employees, George Dowty, left to set up his own company, which went

H.H. Martyn & Co. Ltd factory floor. (David Hanks)

on to become the leading UK manufacturer of aerospace and electrical equipment (more about Dowty later). I have only scratched the surface here but what an astonishing legacy, with much of Martyn's work still in existence for us to enjoy today.

Lister Petter

This Dursley engineering firm was founded in 1867 as R.A. Lister. It is also known simply as Listers and Lister Petter. The company was based in Dursley until 2013 making diesel and petrol engines, one of which was used to power sheep-shearing equipment. Here are a handful of observations from listeners to my radio show that sum up the worldwide impact of this much-loved and treasured company.

Les from Stonehouse worked for Listers for almost fifty years. He said there is not a country in the world where you would not find a Lister engine, adding that they are the most collected engines anywhere. Clive in Gloucester told me how proud he was when visiting a factory in Durban, South Africa, and seeing Lister engines being used. Alec in Gloucester said his uncle found a Lister diesel engine in a Chinese town that helped to pump in the water supply during the Boxer Rebellion, also known as the Boxer Uprising, in northern China between 1899 and 1901. John in Gotherington told us he and his wife saw a Lister butter churn at Disneyland in Florida and felt a pang of homesickness. Pete in Dursley pointed out with pride that his hometown's firm had, at one time, made 95 per cent of the engines used by our fishing fleets.

Dowty

Gloucestershire is teeming with people who either currently or used to work for Dowty, one of the UK's leading innovative engineering companies. It is a global expert in propulsion technology and is famous for designing and manufacturing propellers.

The company was founded in 1931 when George Dowty, an employee at Gloster Aircraft Company, decided to set up on his own and formed the Aircraft Components Company in Cheltenham. The company has had many name changes over the years but the quality and impact of the work has a long legacy.

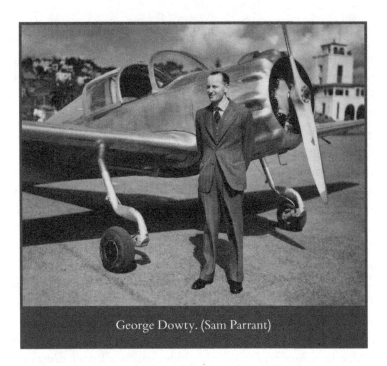

George Dowty. (Sam Parrant)

Gloucestershire's Future

Gloucestershire's heritage of innovation is remarkable and many of today's companies are taking on the challenge of matching their predecessors. The future looks bright knowing so many local businesses will leave their own legacy for future generations to be proud of. A small selection includes:

ZeroAvia based at Cotswold Airport, Kemble, which is revolutionising green air travel.

Global engineering technology group Renishaw, based in Wotton-under-Edge, has been at the forefront of aerospace improvement and is a world leader in robotics and metal 3D printing.

Jones Food Company is transforming the future of farming. It has the world's largest vertical farm and its site in Lydney is the equivalent size of seventy tennis courts.

Innovative underwater research as part of The Deep project at Tidenham Quarry in the Forest of Dean is revolutionising deep sea exploration technology, such as drilling for minerals.

4. CENTRE OF THE UNIVERSE

Centres of Excellence

People come from all over the world to work and play in Gloucestershire because we have become home to many 'centres of excellence'. The list includes:

Fire Service College – On the site of a former RAF station in Moreton-in-Marsh, the Fire Service College was set up in 1968. Fire crews from all over the world train here at the state-of-the-art facility complete with its own fake training motorway, the M96.

270 Climbing Park and Matson Ski Slope – On the outskirts of Gloucester, the park draws in adventurous types from all over the country. It attracts expert climbers in the same way that Matson Ski Slope brings in skiers. Eddie the Eagle spent every hour he could on the slopes at Matson just after it had opened in the 1970s, and look where that led. Eddie and I co-hosted the BBC Radio Breakfast show from these slopes to celebrate the thirtieth anniversary of his Calgary adventure. This kind, funny, crazy friend of mine is loved and admired across the county; I highly recommend *Eddie the Eagle*, the movie starring Taron Egerton, if you haven't already seen it.

Mock M96 motorway used for major incident training.
(Fire Service College)

Co-hosting on the ski slope with Eddie 'the Eagle' Edwards.

GCHQ – GCHQ is the very definition of a centre of excellence, employing more than 6,000 talented people drawn from all over the globe. Those of us who have been around for a while have friends who work there, or as they say, 'I work for the civil service in Cheltenham.' They can't talk about their work despite our botched attempts to trip them up. My dad spent a few months at GCHQ in the 1970s, signed the Official Secrets Act and would never talk about it. Years later I visited the inner sanctum on a press trip and subsequently had the joy of telling my dad I couldn't discuss any of it.

National Star College – There is huge pride across Gloucestershire for this amazing place that started in 1967 and was then known as the Star Centre. Based at Ullenwood Manor above Cheltenham, they provide specialist further education, training, personal development and residential services for people with physical and learning disabilities and acquired brain injuries. As their website states, they are driven by their vision for a world in which people with disabilities are able to realise their potential as equal and active citizens in control of their lives.

Hartpury University and College Campus – This is the top place in the UK for everything equine. Here you will find a world-class equine centre hosting international equestrian events that also teaches equine therapy, rider performance and undertakes industry research. You would expect nothing less from a 'horsy' county.

Headquarters

We have plenty of HQs based in Glorious Gloucestershire and we start with one that might surprise you. When you think of pigeon racing, Huddersfield, Accrington or Scunthorpe may spring to mind rather than the Cotswolds, but we are the Mecca for breeders, fanciers and racers everywhere. As well as being the HQ for the Royal Pigeon Racing Association, we can also claim the Dad's Army Appreciation Society in Stroud, the UK Croquet Association in Cheltenham and Olbas Oil in Gloucester. On that nervy A-level results day, who are you going to call? UCAS, of course. The Universities and Colleges Admissions Service has its HQ in Cheltenham. Also based in Cheltenham are Superdry, Weird Fish and Safran Landing Systems. The Forest of Dean's entry comes from Suntory Ribena in Coleford; Stroud can offer us Ecotricity and Snow Business; while Tewkesbury has Moog, which produces

Stained-glass window at St Peter's Church, Little Rissington, to commemorate the Red Arrows.

electro-hydraulic motion control products. One of Moog's claims to fame is that its technology controls the retractable roof at Wimbledon. We can also boast HQs for GE Aviation, Ecclesiastical Insurance, EDF Energy, the Meningitis Trust and Wall's.

The Red Arrows – Our final HQ deserves a flourish from my listeners, who paint a wonderful picture of what the Red Arrows mean to people in Gloucestershire. The Red Arrows began life at RAF Fairford in 1964, performing their first display at Little Rissington a year later. Pop into St Peter's Church at Little Rissington and the power and the simplicity of the small stained-glass window featuring the Red Arrows will take your breath away.

I have heard many stories from when the crew were based at Kemble Airport and how they used to 'unwind' in the Wild Duck pub at Ewen.

Before they were formed, there was a team called the Red Pelicans based at Little Rissington. Many callers to my show had vivid memories of their dads or husbands flying with that squadron and we managed to link them together to form a Pelicans Reunited group. Other wonderful snippets shared included the fact that the precursor to the Red Arrows was 111 Squadron that operated in the mid-1950s flying Hawker Hunter jets. Many people remembered them practising and often flying over Malmesbury, especially on a Friday. A delivery driver in Kemble told us how he used to stop off and deliver drinks to the Red Arrows boys, who gave him a Red Arrows tie with an image of them in formation. A B&B owner from Bourton-on-the-Hill thought there must be some misunderstanding when a pilot staying with him left a book of stunning Red Arrow photos. It was, of course, a simple gift and much appreciated.

My favourite story came from Sue, who told us about a very happy memory from the 1960s. She was working at a RAF record office in Gloucester and on one occasion went to a dance at RAF Innsworth. She was 17 and went along with her best friend. They met two handsome men, Jim and Rick, who were ground crew. As Sue put it, they always had a good story to tell, well within the Official Secrets Act of the day. The boys would quite happily make the trip from Fairford to Gloucester to meet up with the girls.

5. ARCHITECTURAL INSPIRATIONS

Toddington Manor

I remember the first time I saw the Gothic-style Toddington Manor. I was hiking up the nearby Dumbleton Hill and my walking companion told me to look down to my left and tell me the first thing that came to mind. I saw below me what I thought was the Palace of Westminster. I had to investigate. The house was designed by Charles Hanbury-Tracy and built between 1819 and 1840. Following a fire in 1834, the Houses of Parliament needed to be rebuilt and a competition was held to find a new design. Hanbury-Tracy was chief judge on the competition jury. There is such a resemblance between Toddington Manor and the Houses of Parliament, you can't help but wonder if the winning architect, Charles Barry, had done his homework well and adapted his entry to Tracy's taste. The manor is currently owned by local artist Damien Hirst.

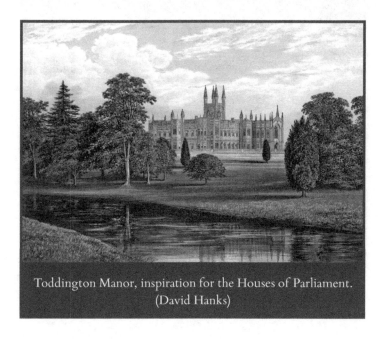

Toddington Manor, inspiration for the Houses of Parliament.
(David Hanks)

Sezincote House

Can you see another architectural similarity – this time between our very own Sezincote House and Brighton Pavilion? It was apparently the Prince Regent's dream to create the Pavilion after he saw Sezincote's wildly over-the-top architecture during a visit to the North Cotswolds. This magical house, built in the Indian Mogul style complete with minarets, was designed by architect Samuel Pepys Cockerell, who was the great-great-nephew of diarist Samuel Pepys. The house and gardens are well worth a visit if you want to learn more about how it captured the Prince Regent's imagination.

Sezincote House.

6. WORDS AND PHRASES INSPIRED BY GLOUCESTERSHIRE

Many of the words and phrases we use every day originate in Gloucestershire. Here is a selection.

William Gilpin was an artist, clergyman, school teacher and author. He was a skilled travel writer and is accredited with being the first person to use the term 'picturesque', meaning 'that kind of beauty which is agreeable in a picture'. It is believed the Wye Valley was his inspiration for the word. He developed a set of rules for the picturesque movement. He said:

> The most perfect river views are composed of four grand parts; the area, which is the river itself; the two side screens which are the opposite banks, the front screen which points out the winding of the river and the ornaments of the Wye … i.e. the ground, rocks, buildings and colour.

Since Glorious Gloucestershire is the most picturesque place on earth, it is rather fitting that the word was inspired by the Wye Valley and Forest of Dean.

Wye Valley View from Symonds Yat Rock.
(Forest of Dean and Wye Valley Tourism)

Gloucestershire's William Tyndale translated the Bible from Orthodox Greek into English and in doing so he enriched the English language by introducing many new words such as 'Passover' and 'scapegoat'. Tyndale also coined familiar phrases such as: 'the powers that be', 'a law unto themselves', 'my brother's keeper', 'a moment in time', 'seek and ye shall find', 'let there be light', 'the salt of the earth', 'signs of the times' and 'the spirit is willing, but the flesh is weak'.

Gloucester-born W.E. Henley's poem 'Invictus' also introduced a couple of famous phrases into our language: 'bloody, but unbowed', 'master of my fate' and 'the captain of my soul'.

I have heard it said that the term 'Beatlemania' came from a newspaper headline the morning after the Fab Four appeared in Cheltenham. This is hotly disputed by those who claim the term was around before the gig, but some really believe that it stems from that night on 3 November 1963. If you read *Beatlemania! The Real Story of The Beatles UK Tours 1963–1965* by Martin Creasy, the Odeon in Cheltenham was the place responsible for that iconic phrase.

Another hotly disputed fact is the origin of the word 'chav'. Did it really come from Cheltenham Ladies' College girls referring to non-college girls as being Cheltenham Average, or men as Cheltenham Mr Average? I personally doubt this one but it is another juicy apocryphal story about the county that we could choose to claim.

How to Squeeze Every Drop Out of Glorious Gloucestershire's Inspirational Inventiveness

Get up early, then complete the following:

Immerse yourself in Gloucestershire's aviation heritage at the Jet Age Museum. This gem is run by a brilliant team of volunteers whose mantra is 'We aim to preserve the past and inspire the future'. They certainly do, and if you want to enjoy this fascinating experience visit the site at the Meteor Business Park on the outskirts of Gloucester.

Next, visit the Jenner museum at Berkeley, climb Nibley Monument, look for the Red Arrows stained-glass window at Little Rissington Church, experience Joe Henson's legacy at the Cotswold Farm Park, pop into Sezincote House, go home and vacuum the house then mow the flippin' lawn, reward yourself with a Budding Ale, nip off to the Mill at Withington for chicken in a basket, then take yourself to bed with a Horlicks.

CUMMINGS' COUNTY QUIZ

ROUND FIVE

1. True or false? A journalist once called me saying that the next day the *Mail on Sunday* were going to report the completely untrue story that I had been kidnapped and held hostage by Laurence Llewelyn-Bowen in Cirencester.

2. New Fancy View is what: the VIP section of the Ivy in Cheltenham with exclusive views over Montpellier, a new locomotive on the extended GWR line to Broadway, or a viewpoint in the Forest of Dean based at an old colliery?

3. In Cheltenham, which came first: the Royal Crescent or the Pittville Pump Rooms?

4. Where is Katharine Lady Berkeley's School?

5. Isambard Kingdom Brunel designed what in Cirencester?

6. Which famous shopping street used to be known as Constitution Way?

7. The magnificent Hidcote Manor Garden is near Chipping Campden, but of what is Hidcote a variety?

8. What insect do you associate most with Selsley Common?

9. Complete the following saying: 'Scratch Gloucestershire and find ...'

10. Which member of the royal family was caught speeding on the A417?

TOUR DE GLOUCESTERSHIRE

THE ULTIMATE BIKE RIDE AROUND GLORIOUS GLOUCESTERSHIRE

FOR CYCLISTS EVERYWHERE, I have devised and ridden a route that will challenge, enthral, educate and delight you. You can squeeze every drop out of Gloucestershire while at the same time squeezing every drop of sweat out of yourself. This can be done in a single day by elite athletes, in two days by pretty fit cyclists, and divided into smaller chunks by everyone else.

Starting the Tour de Glos on the Severn Bridge.

If I were to advertise this ride in a glossy magazine, this is how the advert would go: Our two-day adventure will take you on a trip through time, where you'll visit J.K. Rowling's childhood village and wander around Harry Potter's personal film set. We will take you past ancient castles and iconic abbeys. You'll experience the thrill of winning the Cheltenham Gold Cup and racing down the wing at the home of rugby. You'll visit the exact location where the Domesday Book was signed and marvel at the sensation of standing where kings are buried and battles were fought. This once in a lifetime offer will get your creative juices flowing as you pass through places that gave birth to Scrooge, Long John Silver and the Tailor of Gloucester, as well as landscapes that shaped the work of Dennis Potter and William Shakespeare. The sensations on this trip are unforgettable. You'll enter the world of espionage with some Banksy street art, visit the runway where the B-52s took off for the Gulf War and travel around the cloisters of Gloucester Cathedral.

Our exclusive excursion starts promptly at 7 a.m. on the magnificent Old Severn Bridge, opened by the queen in 1966. We climb high into the Forest of Dean, sweep down into the Severn Vale, lunch at the magnificent Tewkesbury Abbey, and end day one with an ascent into the dreamy North Cotswolds with a visit to Chipping Campden and an overnight stay in Moreton-in-Marsh.

We depart from Moreton promptly on day two at 8 a.m. to capture the magic of many classic Cotswold towns and villages. After a barbecue lunch in Poulton, we make our way to the Roman town of Cirencester, take in Stroud and Frampton on Severn, finishing at the historic Berkeley Castle. Your ending here will be far more joyous than Edward II's, who departed this earth at the castle with the help of a red-hot poker ... allegedly. The price includes transfers, unlimited fresh water, a complementary drink at the Swan Inn at Moreton and a full English breakfast, plus a cool cider at the end of day two.

This fantasy happened in reality on two wheels, in two days, over 200 miles with a gang of inquisitive, cycle-mad friends, and I'd love you to experience the same thrill we enjoyed in an unforgettable exploration of the county. My aim was to create an official route that would highlight the incredible diversity, beauty and history of Gloucestershire. The mix of ingredients included the physical agony that came in the form of Cleeve Hill, the stretches from Chipping

Tour de Glos cyclists reach Cheltenham Race Course.

Campden to Moreton and Selsley Hill. Into the pot we add the magical moments that included cycling around the cloisters at Gloucester Cathedral, along the touchline at Kingsholm and past the finishing post at Cheltenham Racecourse. We enjoyed the sheer beauty of cycling through the Forest of Dean with the River Severn a constant companion, the rolling lavender-scented fun of the North Cotswolds and the homecoming cuddle of the Stroud valleys.

The final element to make this a magnificent experience was simply the people involved along the way. Many just turned up and rode with us, from the Chief Constable who did Northleach to Fairford; Stan from Bream, who did St Briavels to Parkend; Lynette on a trike from Tewkesbury to the racecourse; and Paul from Stroud, who did Selsley to Berkeley Castle. Most of all, we were humbled by the thousands who came out to cheer us along the way; from gentle encouragement in Chepstow at the beginning right through to banners and whistles on Cleeve Hill ... you'll never know how much it meant and helped us.

How to Squeeze Every Drop Out of 'the Tour de Gloucestershire'

Follow the route by copying this link to your browser or Strava app:
www.strava.com/routes/3178833278573422410

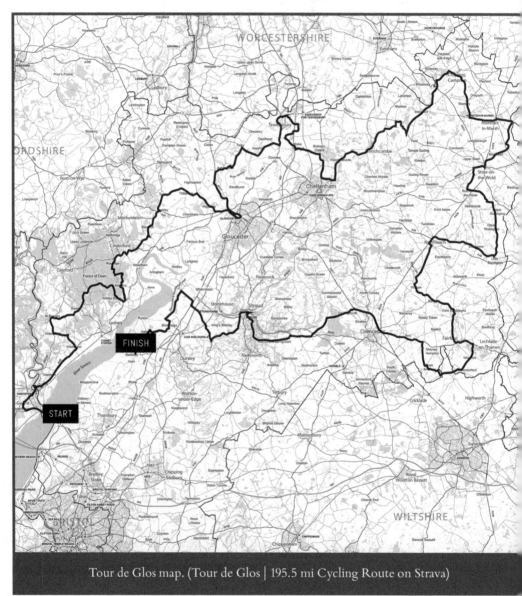

Tour de Glos map. (Tour de Glos | 195.5 mi Cycling Route on Strava)

8

ROCK AND ROLL MAP OF GLOUCESTERSHIRE

GLOUCESTERSHIRE CAN LAY claim to inspiring some of the most recognisable and magical music ever produced. We have provided luxurious homes to rock and pop stars, been the birthplace of classical musical greats and hosted amazing gigs by A-list musicians, albeit in rather curious settings. The line-up for the following fabulous Glorious Gloucestershire festival includes Kylie, Mick Fleetwood, Charlie Watts, Rick Astley, Mike Oldfield, Steve Winwood, Brian Jones, Take That and many more.

BRIAN JONES

Come with me on a ninety-minute rock and roll ramble around Cheltenham. I devised a tour because fans around the world were urging the local council to do more to honour the legacy of native son Brian Jones. Lara Lupin, a diehard fan who lives in Uruguay, even started an online petition. She told me:

> Knowing his legacy inevitably brings us to his roots in Cheltenham. We can't separate Brian Jones from his hometown. For us all over the world there's a need to visit Cheltenham and be able to see the place that influenced him and made him who he was. Cheltenham should tell the world that the true founder of the Rolling Stones was born there.

With the wind in my sails and a merry band of listeners in tow, we set off. Ricky Welch was my trump card. He was a young musician in Cheltenham in the 1960s and kept my tour party spellbound with his insights into the character of the enigmatic Mr Jones. Here is the route we chose:

1. Cheltenham Town Hall. The bust of Brian Jones is currently held here and Ricky told us the story of when he and Brian crept around the back and snuck in to see *the* band of the time called the Ramrods. The Ramrods were part of Brian's rock and roll inspiration and during the 1960s the town hall was the place to see all the great bands.

2. Bath Road (Playhouse theatre). There is a blue plaque stating that Brian lived here. There is another one on Eldorado Road, where he also spent some of his childhood. Ricky mentioned another house in Up Hatherley near the railway line. We shared stories of some of the jobs Brian did in the town, including junior architect, bus conductor, working in a music shop and even delivering coal for a short while. None of these jobs lasted very long.

Brian Jones 'Golden boy' bust, Cheltenham. (Pauline Eccles, CC BY-SA 2.0)

3. 38 Priory Street. This was formerly a secret jazz club. It became very popular with the younger crowd in Cheltenham. Mrs Filby converted her basement into a club for live music, bringing in some of the better-known jazz musicians of the day. Brian quickly became such a frequent visitor that it was practically his second home.

4. Sid Tong's music shop on Winchcombe Street. Ricky used to work here with Brian when he was 16 and Brian was 17. Brian never played any of the instruments in the shop and only took any real interest in Ricky when Ricky bought himself the latest electric guitar.

You could also include Cheltenham cemetery, where Brian was buried after his death in 1969, and the two schools he attended, Dean Close School from September 1949 to July 1953 and Cheltenham Grammar School for Boys (now Pate's Grammar School).

After walking, chatting, sharing stories and learning juicy titbits, we returned to the town hall to sum up what we had learned. I heard about a man who gave very little away about himself, charmed the girls, was a multi-talented musician, could be cold and removed, but also fun (some of my party had once broken into the Lido with him for a late-night dip). He was ambitious and ultimately heartbroken when he felt he had lost control of the Rolling Stones, the band he had formed.

HUBERT PARRY

Whenever I see an aerial shot of the rolling Cotswolds hills bursting with patterns of green and gold there is only one piece of music that enters my head. 'Jerusalem' is the perfect accompaniment to any image of our green and pleasant county. I also happen to have sung it in just about every village hall in Gloucestershire before wild evenings giving talks to the naughty Women's Institute members. We are very proud of the fact that Hubert Parry, the man who composed the music for William Blake's poem, grew up at Highnam Court near Gloucester.

JOHN STAFFORD SMITH

In total contrast, did you know the man who composed 'The Star-Spangled Banner' was also from Gloucestershire? John Stafford Smith was born in Pitt Street in Gloucester in 1750 and baptised in the cathedral. His father was an organist at the cathedral, so it is no surprise that our future composer attended the Cathedral School. The composition was originally written for a private gentlemen's club in England and was only later adapted as the American national anthem. If you visit Gloucester Cathedral you will see the Stars and Stripes flag in the nave. It is placed there to recognise their former pupil's contribution to such an iconic piece of music. On 4 July listen closely as you wander around the city as the cathedral bells will ring out to the sound of 'The Star-Spangled Banner'.

RICK ASTLEY

After his explosion of fame in the 1980s, Rick Astley moved to Rendcomb near Cirencester for a time. I have heard some lovely stories about him from listeners that show the true character of the man. His local postman told me that during a particularly cold miserable winter's day Rick invited him in and gave him a full English breakfast. One of his neighbours told me about the day they were chatting about a Madonna concert in London taking place that night. He told Rick how excited his daughter was to have a ticket and Rick said he was going too and could take her there and back. She was safely delivered home much later that evening after a fantastic show.

JET HARRIS

I got to know Jet Harris quite well as we often drank in the same pub in Gloucester. The former Shadows guitarist had a dry sense of humour and a gentle humility. His greatest anecdote described the rather unusual album he recorded in the city, within the walls of Gloucester Prison, *Inside – Live at Gloucester Prison, 1977*. He recorded it secretly with a band called the Diamonds in the prison chapel, where the acoustics were fantastic. The album was then mixed in a local studio in Stroud and the rest is history.

COZY POWELL

One of the world's greatest rock drummers grew up in Cirencester and nearly caused a major incident when he later returned to perform. Cozy Powell played in the bands Rainbow, Whitesnake and Black Sabbath, and had solo hits with classics such as 'Dance with the Devil'. As a huge Rainbow fan I have loved hearing from his childhood playmates all the stories of what he was like growing up in the town. At the height of his fame he came back for a gig at his old school. He arrived with the full rock and roll kit, a big stack of drums and huge amps and proceeded to blow the school's electrics, leading to the local fire brigade turning up. There is a blue plaque in his honour at the town's Corn Hall, which was unveiled in 2016 by Queen guitarist Brian May, Black Sabbath's Tony Iommi and Suzi Quatro.

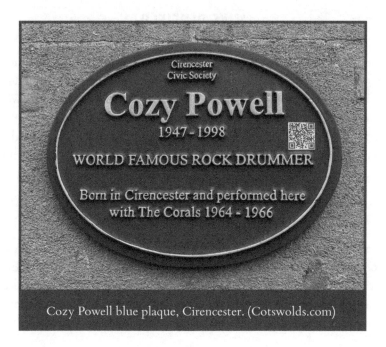

Cozy Powell blue plaque, Cirencester. (Cotswolds.com)

CHARLIE WATTS

Rolling Stones drummer Charlie Watts lived in a classic rock star mansion near Ashleworth, situated halfway between Gloucester and Tewkesbury. The Grade II listed Foscombe House is an imposing Gothic building set in 52 acres of rolling parkland. Charlie converted the coach house into a recording studio for the Stones to record in private. Locals say he was a lovely, kind man. I have no salacious stories of rock and roll excess; the best I can offer is from my mate Andrew, who bumped into Charlie carrying a box of beers to his car in Tesco's car park in Gloucester.

MICK FLEETWOOD

According to his autobiography, Mick did not enjoy growing up at the English boarding schools he attended in the county. He went to King's School, Sherborne House and Wynstones, a Steiner Waldorf school near Gloucester.

MIKE OLDFIELD

In the mid-1970s Mike Oldfield lived at Througham Slad Manor in Bisley above Stroud. This was another huge rock star mansion and my mate Phil taught Mike to fly during his time in Gloucestershire. We are unable to claim to be the inspiration for his classic album *Tubular Bells* as he had written it a few years before moving to the Stroud valleys. Depending on your taste in music, this might not be such a bad thing.

STEVE WINWOOD

One of my all-time musical heroes is Steve Winwood, whose solo work, as well as his music with the bands Traffic and the Spencer Davis Group, has enriched my life considerably. He is based near Northleach, not far from Bourton-on-the-Water, and although we live near each other and occasionally mix in the same circles, I am destined never to meet him. I

Steve Winwood, the idol I am destined never to meet. (Brian Marks, CC BY-SA 2.0)

was due to host 'An Evening with Steve Winwood' at the Roses Theatre in Tewkesbury ahead of an album release but it was cancelled because a last-minute tour came up. I was asked to judge a Bloody Mary drinks competition in the Wheatsheaf Pub in Northleach but passed the honour on to another colleague. He showed me the photos the next day and to my astonishment the bloke standing next to him was Steve Winwood. My mate got squiffy with my hero and didn't even know who the hell he was. I was telling this story of woe to my BBC colleague, Mary, who put the tin lid on it all when she told me Steve used to play the organ in her local church in Northleach at Christmas when she was a child. I give up.

JOHN ENTWISTLE

Gloucestershire does appear to have many fabulous properties that appeal to loaded rock stars. The late Who bass guitarist John Entwistle moved to the seventeen-bedroom Quarwood House near Stow-on-the-Wold in 1978. According to the Stow Civic Society, he was known to walk across the Fosseway and along the footpath, through Maugersbury and up to the Bell in Stow for a drink. The Bell used to have a bar dedicated to John with memorabilia and a jukebox playing only Who classics. He once stood in for the bass player of a local band, the Stowaways, at a fundraising event at the Royal British Legion Club, who were raising money for the Friends of Stow Surgery. It only cost £3 to see the Who legend. John's funeral was held at St Edward's Church in Stow and his ashes were scattered in the grounds of Quarwood.

RALPH VAUGHAN WILLIAMS

A few miles south-east of Cirencester you will find the pretty village of Down Ampney. I cycle through it regularly and each time I hear in my head the strains of Ralph Vaughan Williams's 'Lark Ascending'. It fills me with peace and joy as I trundle through the place of his birth. He was born in the vicarage on 12 October 1872. His father was the Reverend Arthur Vaughan Williams and his mother, Margaret, was Charles Darwin's niece. One of his compositions, the tune to the hymn 'Come down, O love divine', is named 'Down Ampney' and another, titled 'Linden Lea', has been used as a road name in the village as a mark of respect.

Ralph Vaughan Williams.
(CC BY-SA 1.0)

GUSTAV HOLST

Vaughan Williams was a huge fan and inspiration to another Gloucestershire composer who was born in Cheltenham. Gustav Holst is best known for his *Planets* suite but there is so much more to his life and career than this. Williams said about his Gloucestershire neighbour, Holst, 'He was not afraid of being obvious when the occasion demanded, nor did he hesitate to be remote when remoteness expressed his purpose.' Holst's early compositions gave us a clue to the role Gloucestershire would play in his work throughout his life. His *Cotswold Symphony* is a joyful piece hinting at the greatness to come. After leaving Cheltenham Grammar School, he took up the temporary post of organist and choirmaster at Wyck Rissington while conducting the choral society at Bourton-on-the-Water. During this time, he relaxed by hiking all over the Cotswolds Hills. He lived for a time in Cranham and wrote a piece of music there that he entitled 'Cranham'. This was later used for the Christmas carol 'In the Bleak Midwinter'. Subsequently, the cottage he lived in became known as Midwinter Cottage. His former home on Clarence Road is now a wonderful museum. I had the honour of cutting the ribbon when it was refurbished and I highly recommend the music room, where you can see the piano on which he composed *The Planets*.

Statue of Gustav Holst in Imperial Gardens, Cheltenham.

IVOR NOVELLO

Ivor Novello was a singer, composer, actor and dramatist. Part of his childhood schooling was in Gloucester and as a young man he studied under the Gloucester Cathedral organist Sir Herbert Brewer. His name is immortalised in the annual Ivor Novello Awards, which celebrate the very best songwriters and screen composers. It is one of the most-loved and respected music awards you can win. A dear friend of mine has won one and although, like Ivor, he wasn't born here, he found Gloucestershire nearly forty years ago (or did Gloucestershire find him?). Here is a clue to his identity: he wrote songs about a piece of chocolate that is a satisfying treat, a blind man trying to make it to the other side of the road and a girl he urged to build him up because he needed her more than anyone else. These clues should all point you to singer-songwriter Mike d'Abo.

MIKE D'ABO

This lovely man is a music legend who took over from Paul Jones as lead singer with Manfred Mann and had massive hits with 'Mighty Quinn', 'Ha! Ha! Said the Clown', 'My Name is Jack' and many more. He wrote the catchy TV jingle 'A Finger of Fudge' in 1979, which must have worked since so many of us still remember it and can recite the words and tune. Mike, of course, is better known for his classic 'Handbags and Gladrags', first covered by Chris Farlowe but more famously by Rod Stewart and then the Stereophonics. It was used as the theme tune to Ricky Gervais's hit comedy *The Office*.

Mike won his Ivor Novello award for 'Build Me Up Buttercup' and his love of the county is thanks to lyricist Sir Tim Rice, who invited Mike to play in a charity cricket match in Coln St Aldwyns near Bibury. Mike immediately became besotted with the county, moved here, fell in love with his third wife Lisa, settled in the Stroud valleys and started a young family. We became close friends while working on the radio together and I feel it is my obligation to spill the beans about my mad, loveable, crazy pal. When your early life's experiences are schooling at Harrow, followed by studying theology at Cambridge, nearly ending up

Sharing a 'Finger of Fudge' with Mike d'Abo.

in the ministry but instead becoming a famous pop star in the swinging Sixties, you will have an interesting view of the world and relationship with reality.

I was the best man at his wedding to Lisa and I spent the first ten minutes scrounging cash from the invited crowd because he had forgotten to pay the registrar, who wouldn't start the ceremony without her money. When the concept of 'cash back' in shops was first introduced, Mike struggled with the notion. Sent off to do the shopping in a local supermarket in Stroud, he came back with a huge grin and placed fifty quid on the kitchen table. He declared that the competition between stores must be intensifying as they were now giving away free cash. Over lunch one day I asked him what he was doing that night. He told me, and the rest of the pub, that he would be appearing as a guest on *This is Your Life* for Paul Jones. I gently raised the obvious point, 'Aren't you supposed to keep that a closely guarded secret and tell no one, especially a journalist like me?' He looked a bit hurt and told me he trusted me!

In that same pub, with the rest of the customers listening, he also told me in excruciating detail about every twist and turn of the recent reversal of his vasectomy … and I was eating spaghetti bolognese. The procedure obviously worked because his wife Lisa gave birth to twins Ella and Louis, named after Ella Fitzgerald and Louis Armstrong, a year or so later.

JOE MEEK

We have the Forest of Dean to thank for Radio 2 DJs, Eurovision stars, 1990s indie bands and one of the most influential music producers ever. Joe Meek was born at No. 1 Market Square, Newent, where you will see a blue plaque dedicated to the man who wrote and recorded the ground-breaking tune 'Telstar'. This was the first British record to be number one on both sides of the Atlantic. Joe introduced the music business to innovative production techniques like sampling and overdubbing that are still used today. His life came to a tragic end when, in debt, fighting copyright litigation and sinking into depression, he shot his landlord and then took his own life.

JIMMY YOUNG AND CINDERFORD

Leslie Ronald Young was born in Woodside Street in Cinderford and attended St White's Primary School and East Dean Grammar School. You might know him better as DJ Jimmy Young, who had a top career in the 1950s as a crooner before entertaining the nation on national radio for decades.

Cinderford also provided us with the 1990s alternative rock band EMF (unbelievable I know). Lead singer of Years and Years, actor and Eurovision star Olly Alexander grew up in Coleford, and the Verve's Richard Ashcroft owns Taynton House, which was built in 1660 and features a period bullring, secret garden and ornamental pond.

CLEARWELL CASTLE

The Forest of Dean can also claim to be the location where great albums were written and recorded. Bands such as Led Zeppelin, Badfinger, Deep Purple, Queen, Whitesnake, Mott the Hoople, Bad Company and Black Sabbath chose Clearwell Castle as their base to create chaos, magic and great rock and roll. The iconic album *Sabbath Bloody Sabbath* was created here. Ozzy and the gang had struggled for inspiration in LA but found their muse after spending time in the scary dungeons.

THE BEATLES IN GLOUCESTERSHIRE

The Sub Rooms in the heart of Stroud is the place to go for all Beatles fans. For a band so universally loved, it is quite refreshing to gain an insight into the tough early years and the reality of trying to get that first big break. They appeared at the Sub Rooms on 31 March 1962 and, as Sir Paul McCartney said, 'Stroud was pretty bad ... We'd never heard of it, but we went there and I think about three people showed up.' Over the years I have spoken to many who were there that night and it has gone down in local folklore. It was Pete Best on the drums at that time. They got about £30 for the gig and had to endure a bunch of Teddy Boys throwing coins at them. They did come back in the September and had a slightly better experience, and of course the following month they released 'Love Me Do' and the rest is pop history. The Sub Rooms is a fantastic venue and you will still find the original posters there plus a wonderful café and bar, local beers and great gigs in the ballroom where the Beatles once played.

The Beatles also played at Lydney Town Hall, the Odeon in Cheltenham and the Regal in Gloucester. My favourite Beatles story is from journalist Hugh Worsnip, who was working for *The Citizen* newspaper in Gloucester at the time. It was March 1963 when the Beatles came to the city as a support act for American heartthrobs Chris Montez and Tommy Roe, and Hugh turned up beforehand to suss out the action. Two men walked up to him and asked if he would interview them and give their band some publicity. He was busy at the time but said he would seek them out later if they wrote their names down in his note-pad. The names in his pad were John Lennon and Paul McCartney.

Poster advertising the Beatles at the Subscription Rooms, Stroud.

TENUOUS BUT TRUE

Here is where I scrape the barrel of Gloucestershire's musical links but I think you will appreciate the stories.

Kylie Minogue

Genealogists have claimed that Kylie's clan are related on her mother's side to Dinah Riddiford, who was probably the oldest woman to swing from the gallows at Gloucester gaol. She and her son were jailed for the theft of various cuts of meat. Her son, Luke, was sent to the penal colonies in Australia, while she was hung in public.

Michael Jackson

The King of Pop wrote a song about Gloucestershire that I have heard many times and I can assure you that it doesn't get better after a few plays. He was great friends with the child actor Mark Lester, who played Oliver Twist in the screen adaptation. Mark is based in Cheltenham and Jackson, godfather to Mark's children, often stayed here. The song is called 'Days in Gloucestershire', but Michael can't pronounce the word Gloucestershire. Download it for a giggle because it is truly awful.

Liam Gallagher

In 2008 Liam Gallagher took a moody stroll around the Model Village in Bourton-on-the-Water while filming the video for the Oasis track 'I'm Outta Time'. Take a look on YouTube. He swaggers into the village two minutes and ten seconds into the song.

Alvin Stardust

He of the leather glove and 'My Coo Ca Choo' fame's son, Shaun, was head teacher at Pate's Grammar School in Cheltenham. There is nothing more to say.

BEFORE THEY WERE FAMOUS

Gloucestershire has hosted some of the biggest names in music at some of the unlikeliest of venues.

Oasis played at Gloucester Leisure Centre in 1995. They had just become beyond massive with the album *Definitely Maybe* but had signed the contract with the venue before the band's fame had exploded and tickets were £10.

Approximately sixty turned up to see U2 in 1980 at the Marshall Rooms in Stroud. The following bands played at the following venues: Radiohead at the Guildhall in Gloucester; Fleetwood Mac at the Bristol Hotel in Gloucester; the Prodigy at a rave in a field near Bibury; Vanilla Ice at Gloucester Leisure Centre; Take That at Lakers School in the Forest of Dean; Queen at Cheltenham Town Hall; Whitesnake at the Orepool Inn near Coleford; and Rod Stewart, Elton John, David Bowie and Eric Clapton played at the Blue Moon Club in Cheltenham.

How to Squeeze Every Musical Drop Out of Glorious Gloucestershire

Try the Gustav Holst Way from Cranham to Wyck Rissington via Cheltenham and Bourton-on-the-Water. Take your time and do it over a period of days as it is a decent 35-mile adventure. Download your favourite Holst pieces including the 'Cotswold Symphony', strap on some sturdy walking boots and discover the Cotswold countryside that inspired such great works. Everything you need, including guide books, is available online.

Take a moment to sit quietly in Gloucester Cathedral and enjoy the choir, reflect on the centuries of music shared and talent developed here, including Ivor Novello and John Stafford Smith.

Take a walk in Highnam Woods to the strains of 'Jerusalem' in honour of Sir Hubert Parry. If you go early in the morning or at dusk you will have a great chance of hearing the native nightingales.

Take a leisurely bike ride through Down Ampney and look for Linden Lea Road, named in honour of Ralph Vaughan Williams's work.

Wander around Cheltenham guided by the information in this chapter to gain a real sense of the formative years of Brian Jones.

Book the Mermaid Suite at Clearwell Castle and claim you have shared the same room as Freddie Mercury.

CUMMINGS' COUNTY QUIZ

ROUND SIX

1. True or false? Ecotricity boss and Forest Green Rovers chairman Dale Vince is well known for his hippy roots. He had a minor role dressed as a druid in the video of the Kate Bush hit 'Running Up That Hill'.

2. Cheltenham-born Richard O'Brien wrote which classic cult musical show?

3. The late A.A. Gill referred to which Cotswold town as being 'The worst place in the world'?

4. Which bird do you associate with Symonds Yat Rock?

5. Who owns Snowshill Manor Gardens?

6. What mouth-watering cargo used to come up the Gloucester Sharpness canal from Frampton on Severn to a special place near Birmingham?

7. Is Painswick a town or a village?

8. To what does the following Cotswold phrase from the past refer: 'He had teeth curled and his ears pinned further back.' Is it a description of someone who is drunk, smartened up or aggressive?

9. ARRC are stationed at Imjin Barracks, what does ARRC stand for?

10. For what product is GR Lane in Gloucester most famous?

9

ECCENTRIC GLOUCESTERSHIRE

GLOUCESTERSHIRE IS WELL known for bizarre and wacky pursuits. I have been so lucky to have been involved in all of the following exploits in one way or another and I am a better person for it. If there are any you haven't experienced why not commit to spectating or partaking in at least one? You won't regret it.

THE ASSIZE OF ALE

Breathe deeply because I am about to paint a rather alarming image of Gloucestershire at its most bizarre. I need to use a very long sentence to do it justice. Here goes: I was sitting in a Gloucester pub wearing a medieval costume watching a man in leather trousers being slapped on the bottom by a rather giddy lady just before he sat on a stool covered in beer and I thought, 'I love this county'. I am part of gang of scallywags and nincompoops who re-enact a quirky historic tradition that involves a city's sheriff testing the quality of ale with a wooden stool, leather breeches and an egg timer. The Assize of Ale dates back to medieval times, when the sheriff was responsible for ensuring the ale in the city was of 'palatable quality'. This is where the 'Ale Conner' comes in. His job is to pour some beer on to a stool, then sit on it in his leather breeches for three minutes. If he stands up with ease the beer has passed the test. If the leather sticks to the ale and the stool comes up with him then this

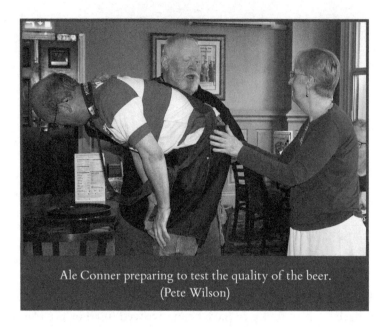

Ale Conner preparing to test the quality of the beer.
(Pete Wilson)

is where the trouble starts. This indicates too much sugar in the ale and, keep in mind, this test began at a time when there was a sugar tax. The sheriff could immediately close down the pub and put the landlady 'on the game', according to Gloucester Town Crier Alan Myatt. To honour the tradition, we visit about twenty pubs collecting for charity and perform the test in every one to the great amusement, confusion and sheer incredulity of the locals. If you want to squeeze every drop out of Gloucestershire and every drop of ale out of the Ale Conner's breeches then join us every autumn on our historical pub crawl.

WASSAILING

Look out in January for your local wassail. It is a traditional, luck-bringing custom with singing, Morris dancing, drama and a parade of beasts including a bull figure effigy with horns. People surround the apple trees in local orchards, where cider is poured over the roots of the trees to ward away evil spirits and ensure a good harvest.

SEVERN BORE

The Severn bore, a tidal surge, can be witnessed throughout the year, although spring and autumn often see the biggest waves. Look out for four- or five-star Severn bores and watch the surfers. Check for details on severn-bore.co.uk

MAY MADNESS

May is a crazy month and I love it. It starts with May Day Morris Dancing on May Hill and Painswick Beacon. I have hosted my show at both locations and I can't begin to tell you how magical this experience is. If your weather app is promising you a decent morning, set your alarm and get up there for 4.30 a.m.

May Day on May Hill.

I love taking people for a visit to the top of May Hill. I wish I could bottle their reaction when they first see the view of the snaking River Severn and enjoy the sense of peace and calm among the clump of trees planted to commemorate Queen Victoria's Golden Jubilee. This is my happy place and if you have never been to the top, give it try. You won't regret it.

RANDWICK WAP

It has been a great honour to be involved with this lovely community who keep their local traditions alive in the most wonderful way. The celebrations begin on the first Sunday in May in this tiny village high up above Stroud. The newly appointed Wap Queen and Village Mayor take centre stage in a procession to the village pool, where they are anointed. After that, three Double Gloucester cheeses are hurled down the steep slope of the churchyard.

Randwick Wap. (Matt Bigwood, *Stroud Times*)

MARKING DAY

This is the day when the cows are released onto Minchinhampton Common. The name comes from when livestock owners would gather with their animals beside the Old Lodge (now a pub) on Minchinhampton Common and each cow would be tagged or marked before being released. The cattle roam free on the commons for the summer.

ST BRIAVELS BREAD AND CHEESE DOLE

Every Whit Sunday, bread and cheese is blessed by the vicar and thrown from the wall outside the church for the assembled crowd of waiting 'Dole Claimers' to collect. Some believe the morsels have mysterious preservative properties and keep them as a lucky charm.

CHEESE ROLLING

This takes place on Spring Bank Holiday at Coopers Hill near Gloucester. Get there early, perch on the hill and let the madness begin.

TETBURY WOOLSACK RACING

On the same weekend as cheese rolling, you can watch the poor teams carrying a 60lb woolsack for the men's race and a 35lb one for the women's race up and down Gumstool Hill, which has a 1 in 4 gradient.

COTSWOLD OLIMPICK GAMES

Held on the Friday after Spring Bank Holiday on Dover's Hill near Chipping Campden, Robert Dover's Cotswold Olimpick Games date back to 1612. Enjoy the Shin-kicking, Tug O' War, and a series of events to become Champion of the Hill that include the Static Jump (jumping as far as possible from a standstill) and Spurning the Barre (an old English version of the Scottish tossing the caber).

How to Squeeze Every Drop of Madness and Merriment out of Glorious Eccentric Gloucestershire

During the summer look out for the elver eating and sheep racing in Frampton on Severn, scarecrow festivals all over the county, and don't miss the teams at Bourton-on-the-Water thrashing through the River Windrush in the famous football match on August Bank Holiday.

The first Saturday in September brings us the Mock Mayor of Barton being paraded through the city in a ridiculous contraption for Gloucester Day. Historically this is also when the Newent Onion Eating Fayre takes place, so check out if it is happening. The Gloucester Day procession is shortly followed by the previously mentioned Assize of Ale, and if you still have the energy for something daft why not take your dog to Sandford Park Lido in October? This magnificent outdoor pool in Cheltenham allows you to bring your pooch for a dip the day before they shut for the winter and clean out the pool.

Finally, if you reach the end of the year and still feel the need for a life-affirming, barmy day out, why not head to Bibury on Boxing Day for the duck racing. This has grown so big that the little yellow rubber duck race on the River Coln has gone global and is live-streamed around the world.

It is with great pride that I say Gloucestershire folk are cheese-chasing, elver-eating, shin-kicking, onion-scoffing, duck-racing, Morris-dancing nincompoops … and proud of it.

Lavender Fields at Snowshill (affectionately known as Snozzle). (Cotswolds Tourism, Cotswolds.com)

Mock Mayor's *Titanic* impression on entering Tewkesbury.

Sezincote House, inspiration for the Brighton Pavilion.

In Mike d'Abo's music studio.

Stained-glass window at Little Rissington to commemorate the Red Arrows.

Magical, mysterious Puzzlewood. (Wye Valley and Forest of Dean Tourism)

Fern Ticket – cut out and keep.

Entrance to Tolkien's world at St Edward's
Church, Stow-on-the-Wold.
(Cotswolds Tourism, Cotswolds.com)

Mock Mayor supporting Gloucester in the Shed at Kingsholm.

Star Wars Stormtroopers surfing the Seven bore.
(Wye Valley and Forest of Dean Tourism)

Leaving a legacy through the generations, Adam and Joe Henson.

Gladys' Leap – tribute to Cranham's Gladys Hillier, who jumped a stream to deliver the post.

Mirror in Charlton Kings that inspired Lewis Carroll's *Through the Looking-Glass*. (David Elder)

The view that inspired Ivor Gurney's yearning for the Severn and May Hill from the trenches.

Ale Conner preparing to test the quality of the beer with Gloucester Town Crier Alan Myatt.

10

BRINGING HISTORY BACK TO LIFE

MY YEAR AS MOCK MAYOR

WHEN I BEGAN my roller coaster ride of a radio career, the one piece of advice I was given over and over from the veterans in my profession was, 'keep moving so they can't shoot you'. The art of survival was to host a show for a couple of years, then scarper to another radio station before they found you out. I took this pearl of wisdom literally, hence when I turned up on the doorstep of BBC Radio Gloucestershire begging for a contract, I had already worked at nine stations. Then a strange thing happened. An internal voice kept telling me this was a very special place and maybe I should hang around for a while. My epiphany happened in a smoke-filled room in a pub on Barton Street in Gloucester when I was handed a scroll that I still have on my wall to this day. The scroll was presented to me by the Mayor of Barton inviting me into his 'Court Leet' to take on the role of 'Merlin the Magician to the Court Leet of Barton St Mary'. At this moment I realised I had been invited into a special world full of kind, eccentric, loving people and Gloucestershire was the only place I wanted to stay. Subsequently we bought a house, had children and threw ourselves into every aspect of life offered to us here, and not a day goes by when I am not grateful for finding such a fantastic place to call home.

Newly appointed Mock Mayor of Barton.

The history of the role of the Mock Mayor of Barton and its reinvention in the 1980s epitomises the uniqueness and humour of where we live. It all started when Charles II was returned to the throne in 1660. He didn't like Gloucester very much, because its inhabitants had sided with Cromwell during the English Civil War and had successfully withstood a famous siege, refusing entry to a force commanded by the new king's father. Once the monarchy was restored, Charles took his revenge in various ways, including knocking down the city walls, and severely reducing the city boundaries. This left the Barton area on the outside of the city. The residents didn't like *that* very much, and decided that, if they couldn't defer to the Mayor of Gloucester, then they would invent their own, simply to poke fun at Gloucester's official powers that be. Originally, the man who was judged to have made the biggest fool of himself during the preceding year was given the honour of being appointed Mock Mayor of Barton. The office fell into disuse in mid-Victorian times but it was revived at the end of the twentieth century by the Barton Residents Association in an attempt to improve the quality of life in this area of the city. Since then we have had an eccentric and eclectic mix of characters in the role all representing the spirit of rebellion, mickey taking and altruism. Having done some amateur prestidigitation in my time, the Court Leet decided my conjuring skills should be put to good use and so my magical association with them began.

In 2017 I was summoned as we prepared to elect the new Mock Mayor. You can imagine my shock when it was revealed that the new Mock Mayor was to be me. I knew instantly that the following year would be hectic, funny, weird, moving and very bad for my liver. I vowed to serve with all my heart and keep the spirit of rebellion and mischief-making going for every second of the next twelve months and squeeze every drop of life out of this historic role.

My first duty was to buy everyone a pint in the Court Leet's regular pub, One Eyed Jacks on Barton Street. It was a rowdy, raucous night. The Mock Mayor must be officially appointed in the Barton area and so a little while later I was back at One Eyed Jacks surrounded by my Court Leet, friends, family and several pints of ale for the ceremony. The speeches, proclamations, abuse and mickey taking all merged into one riotous party. I am not sure quite how I made it on air for my breakfast show at 6 a.m. the next morning but I am told that I did.

Mock Mayor with his Court Leet outside
One Eyed Jacks pub.

Part two happened a couple of days later when, in full regalia of red robes, a chain fashioned from a lavatory chain and a tricorn hat, I ventured into the Shed for Gloucester's first game of the season. This isn't a place for the faint hearted but I decided the Mock Mayor should be there. This was one of the most memorable nights at Kingsholm with a jam-packed, full-to-the-brim stadium, a gutsy, thrilling, tight tussle and to cap it off a last-minute win over champions Exeter. The city was buzzing that night and the energy and afterglow spread into the next day, which was Gloucester Day. This is held to celebrate the victory in the Siege of Gloucester and it starts with the Mock Mayor being paraded around the city in some comedy contraption. Over the years there have been wheelie bins, rubber dinghies, tricycles and for me, my loving Court Leet provided a sedan chair ... without a chair. It looked like something crossed between a *Carry On* movie and an episode of *The Flintstones*.

Gloucester Day procession.

I wore a permanent smile for the whole day, lapping up the eccentricity, humour and warmth from thousands of people. It genuinely was one of the most memorable, touching, emotional days of my life. These crazy capers continued throughout the year to ensure the Mock Mayor role and its historical heritage stays alive and thrives. The people of Barton welcomed me into their world and in 2017 gave me the ultimate gift. In a community of more than fifty nationalities and different languages, the theme of acceptance and integration was a story I vowed to highlight for the next twelve months.

I was determined to use my role of 'the bloke off the radio' to show the Barton I knew and loved to the wider audience. Having discovered there were lots of Bartons all over Gloucestershire, I decided a week-long pilgrimage from one Barton to the next was needed. I was quite nervous as I headed out of Barton Street in Gloucester on the Monday morning of my Barton to Barton week. The concept was quite ambitious. Day one took us to Barton Hill in the Forest of Dean and then on to Barton Street in Tewkesbury. That night I hosted a history quiz in the Royal Hop Pole pub between members of my Court Leet and the Tewkesbury Medieval Society. The drinks were flowing that night. We had two town criers trying to outdo each other and the Gloucester contingent recreated history by showing how to test the quality of the ale by sitting on a beer-drenched stool in leather trousers. By the time I had mixed the teams up I had lost all control of proceedings. There was a lovely moment when the Tewkesbury team started singing a local medieval song, only for the Gloucester team to respond with a rendition of 'We are the Gloucester Boys', which included the lines:

Maggie dear, a pint of beer, a woodbine and a match
A Tuppenny ha'penny stick of rock, we're off to the rugby match
To see ol' Glo'ster score a try, the best try in the land.

We live in a truly welcoming part of the world. There was no greater example of this than when, dressed in full Mock Mayor's outfit, I entered the hamlet of Barton in between Guiting Power and Kineton flanked by two former Mock Mayors after a 20-mile walk from Tewkesbury via Oxenton, Winchcombe and Guiting Woods. Our hosts Alex and Hattie had invited the neighbours round and opened up their luxurious home and gardens to a raggle taggle bunch of nitwits, who drank all their beer and wine, scoffed every corn-flavoured snack going and proceeded to make ourselves very much at home. It was a splendid evening where two very different worlds met, got on well, explored our shared experiences, found many things in common and agreed to stay in touch. Just behind Alex and Hattie's stunning property is Barton Bank, inspiration for the name of the famous race horse. There is also a very special area called Barton Bushes at the back of Adam Henson's Cotswold Farm Park and he gave us a piece of his dry-stone wall for a sensory garden we were building back in Gloucester at the time.

I wanted the children from St James' School in Barton to come and meet the children from Innsworth School. There are many nationalities represented at both schools, including Nigeria, Latvia, Poland and Greece. The Barton Street children had prepared a board with images such as mosques, Mock Mayors, exotic food shops and the City Farm. They pointed out with great pride the parts of their patch they loved the most. The Innsworth children were totally engrossed and fired off endless questions, wanting to know more about their lives and culture. I captured every moment for a radio broadcast and will cherish the recordings forever.

Of course, it would have been impossible to traverse the Cotswolds without some theatrics during my Barton to Barton week, so I canoed across the Severn from Arlingham to Newnham and did a *Titanic* performance à la Kate Winslet on the bow of a boat approaching Tewkesbury. I nearly killed myself on an electric fence near Winchcombe, and at Barton Abbots in Tetbury I raced down the road in my sedan chair. The Tetbury Lions are a group of fun-loving locals who always help out when needed. They love life and have exactly the same attitude to enjoying it as my Court Leet. With the help of the local police, they closed the road and recreated their famous Wacky Races event by providing a professional commentator, a loudspeaker and a go-kart to race against me. I trundled up and down in the 'sedan' chair I had used to parade through the Streets of Gloucester a year previously. They could hear us as far away as Avening, Cherrington and Nailsworth.

Our gift to all the friends we made along the way was a Barton Baton. A simple rolled-up scroll, tied with a red ribbon and a message of friendship from one Barton to another. One of my favourite nights was our

Presentation of the Barton Baton scroll.

final fling at the fittingly named Barton End. I hosted a local knowledge quiz in a farmer's back garden between a slightly intoxicated Court Leet of Barton St Mary and a sober and competitive gang from this pretty hamlet up the hill from Nailsworth. Our host, Roland, made the school-boy error of offering my lot a free go at his alcohol stash and as it had been a long week they demolished it with relish. As had happened all week, it only took about half an hour before the other Bartons decided they liked my friends' fun-loving vibe and joyfully came down to our level with alcohol consumption and ribald behaviour. A riotous night ensued with batons exchanged, friendships born and commitments made for a reciprocal visit. Carlton Green, who came to Gloucester from Jamaica in the 1950s, ended up chatting to an old friend he hadn't seen in years. They both worked at the Daniels engineering firm in Stroud many moons ago and I later heard that when Carlton got home very late that night he was on such a high he couldn't sleep.

Those twelve months sum up what an incredible county Gloucestershire is in so many different ways. People who live here do not only preserve history, they bring it back to life in the silliest, most life-enhancing way.

High-flying Mock Mayor making
the most of his year in office.

How to Squeeze a Little History out of Glorious Gloucestershire

On the first Saturday in September head to Gloucester and enjoy Gloucester Day. The Gate Streets are alive with stalls, stands, historical and hysterical street performances and all the pomp and ceremony of the traditional parade through the city led by the Mayor and Sheriff of Gloucester in full civic regalia. This day has been celebrated for centuries to commemorate the lifting of the Siege of Gloucester in 1643. The highlight for me is always the comic meeting of the Mock Mayor of Barton with the real Mayor of Gloucester. Believe me, the ritual that follows as the Mock Mayor is officially appointed will blow your mind.

CUMMINGS' COUNTY QUIZ

ROUND SEVEN

1. True or false? If you look at the final building at the end of the Municipal Offices in Cheltenham near Neptune's Fountain, it appears to be part of the whole run of buildings. Look more closely and you will spot a modern addition 'suggested' by an amateur architect from Tetbury, also known as King Charles III.

2. The Fosse Way runs through Gloucestershire and ends in Lincoln, but where does it begin?

3. On which river does Cirencester stand?

4. Which name is a place in the Cotswolds near Cirencester and another place 151 miles north where Michael Parkinson and Dicky Bird come from?

5. What is the highest point in the Cotswolds?

6. What is the origin of the name Blakeney in the Forest of Dean: the farmstead of the Blake family, the dark-coloured island in the marsh, or the pathway to the sandbank of Sabrina?

7. Which comedy filmed in the county has the fictional pub the Keepers Arms?

8. Which is furthest north up the Severn, Lydney or Longney?

9. Which of the following places really exists: Bunch of Nuts, Goosy Gander Copse or Charley Farley Hillock?

10. In 1866 a lifeboat was launched into which well-known place: the Gloucester-Sharpness Canal at Slimbridge, the River Avon at Tewkesbury or Pittville Lake in Cheltenham?

11

FUN AND GAMES
WITH PLACE NAMES

LET ME TAKE you on a little journey, stopping off at Nanny Farmer's Bottom on our way to Paradise via The Heavens. These are all real places in Gloucestershire and I want to share with you some of the stories behind the famous and less famous names in the county. We will find out about local nicknames, hear why the Slaughters is nothing to worry about and learn some Gloucestershire rhyming slang (which rivals the Cockney version). We will explore the stories such as a crossing place that inspired the title of a Fairport Convention album. I will introduce you to some local characters: Algernon Toadsmore, Bartholomew Cockadilly, Dixie Dumbleton and Dr James Slimbridge, who are all ready to star in a Dame Jilly Cooper novel.

Armed with a little local knowledge, it is a wonderful feeling to casually drop a little nugget into conversations here and there. It always impresses the recipient, makes you feel good and spreads the word about our amazing county. Whether you have lived here all your life, chosen Gloucestershire as your home or are just visiting, I am sure you will enjoy learning a little more. We will start by finding out how some of our place names can be reinvented.

THE GLOUCESTERSHIRE VERSION OF *THE MEANING OF LIFF*

One of my favourite books is *The Meaning of Liff* by Douglas Adams and John Lloyd. They have a theory that there are many experiences, feelings, situations and objects for which there is currently no single word, but there are plenty of place names that would happily fit the bill. People from all over the county helped to create the Gloucestershire version for my radio show. I hope you enjoy these examples:

North Nibley – the fizzy feeling before you sneeze.

Ozleworth – the blissful feeling after you have sneezed.

Temple Guiting – the sensation of total peace during meditation.

Cheltenham – the smug look worn by someone who knows they are right.

Minsterworth – the overenthusiastic member of a congregation.

The Pludds – the impending sense of doom having scoffed a vindaloo.

Frampton – the lingering unpleasant smell no one can find a reason for or own up to.

Dinglewell – the scraggy bit on the Sellotape you try and pull up to get it moving again.

Matson – the guilty look on a dog's face when they have been in the kitchen bin.

Bibury – the smile on the face of a member of the WI when you crack a rather near-the-knuckle gag. They think it's funny but are not prepared to laugh out loud in case their mates are not amused.

Chedworth – unit of currency in a bartering system using cheese.

Birdlip – a cheeky parrot.

Longlevens – a wonderful lie-in.

Hucclecote – a little Norman Wisdom-type trip.

Uley – feeling in need of a pint.

Cinderford – an amorous adventure in a motor vehicle with someone other than your partner or spouse! Derived from early French *sin de ford*, which also means 'nookie' on the riverbank.

Dymock – how you feel when you trip up a kerb or walk into a lamppost and realise someone saw you do it.

Adlestrop – that annoying feeling you get when you just can't quite think of the appropriate word to describe something.

Tirley – that spinny thing that appears when your internet is weak and you can't download something.

Pinfarthings (a hamlet near Amberley) – the tiny globule of spit that leaves your mouth and to your horror, lands on the cheek of the person opposite at a social event. You don't know them well enough to wipe it off and apologise, so it remains there glistening back at you.

COLLOQUIAL NAMES EXPLAINED

Many Gloucestershire places have intriguing names with a fascinating backstory. Here are some of the best:

Gladys' Leap. This has to be my favourite of any tale linked to a curious place name. Gladys Hillier delivered post to the people of Cranham for thirty-five years but there was one household that was a little tricky to reach. The Coopers' house was bordered by a brook and to access the property Gladys had to walk over a wooden plank that straddled the water. The plank would often be dislodged and float away, but instead of taking a long detour, Gladys would leap across the challenging 3ft 'crevasse' with her heavy mail bag. When she retired, the village celebrated the service of this Cranham-born legend and her daily leap over the brook was mentioned in one of the speeches. The story caught the attention of the Ordnance Survey people and the grid reference was noted and marked on all future maps. It can be found at SO 8906 1206. I recently put Gladys' Leap into Google Maps and it took me straight there. It is well worth a visit for a little adventure. The British folk rock group Fairport Convention also heard the story and named their 1985 album *Gladys' Leap*.

Granny's Pumps. I have driven past the layby on the A417 just north of the Highwayman Pub more than 8,000 times. It was my daily commute into work and I have only recently discovered that it is known as 'Granny's Pumps'. The layby apparently gets its name from a petrol station that was there up until the early 1960s and was run by an elderly woman. The pumps were hand operated and she would be there through thick and thin to fill up motorists on their journey north.

Gladys' Leap at Cranham.

Hetty Pegler's Tump.

Hetty Pegler's Tump. Hetty Pegler's Tump, officially known as the Uley Long Barrow, is a partially reconstructed Neolithic burial mound, at least 5,000 years old, overlooking the Severn Valley. It measures 121ft long, 112ft wide and its height is just under 10ft. It is known locally as Hetty Pegler's Tump, after the woman who owned the land in the seventeenth century. The first time I crawled into this magical labyrinth of stone-built tunnels I had quite a shock. There were two women down one of the chambers smoking weed and on hearing my voice they told me they were both avid listeners of my radio show. I have been back several times for a more sedate visit and can thoroughly recommend it.

POWER TO THE PEOPLE

Many street names, school names and road signs are linked to famous people but who were they? Two schools in Stroud are named after famous local men: former MP Samuel Stevens Marling was the person who put up most of the money for the creation of Marling School and Thomas Keble was a long-serving nineteenth-century vicar in Bisley. Tom Long's post can be seen at the crossroads on Minchinhampton Common. The romantic view is that he was a highwayman who was hanged there but it is considered far more likely that he was a local suicide buried out of town on non-consecrated ground.

Tom Long's Post.

The street named after a local character that amuses me the most is an underwhelming road opposite the Golden Farm pub on the Beeches estate in Cirencester called Herbert Stark Close. Many of my listeners filled me in on this one as it involves a chap who they all knew very well and loved. He was a true eccentric who, rumour had it, was very rich but lived an alternative lifestyle. He used to walk around Cirencester in the late 1970s looking like the archetypal homeless person. He wore a scruffy black suit, a dishevelled hat and always had a flower in his lapel. He used to wheel along an old black butcher's pushbike, which he would decorate for special occasions. He lived at the bottom of Victoria Road and he always had a good word for everybody.

You may have driven along Tommy Taylor's Lane in Cheltenham but do you know who he was? Some people think he was a local boxing promoter but the earliest records date back much further and lead us to a map from 1884 showing a Taylor's Lane, probably named after a local landowner.

Dr Newton's Way, a ring road around Stroud, was named after the very popular local Dr Newton, whose practice was the Chestnuts at the top of Hollow Lane from the 1930s to the 1960s.

Here are some examples of other interesting inspiration for road names: Lobleys Drive in Abbeymead in Gloucester is named after Lobley's farm. Nearby Heron Way was named after the housebuilder, and to keep the theme going all the other roads nearby were named after birds. Abbeydale and Abbeymead are so called because of Prinknash Abbey. Hare Lane in Gloucester derives from the Old English name for a military road. Black Jack Street in Cirencester is named after a statue of St John the Baptist that became discoloured. Coldharbour Road in St Briavels in the Forest of Dean is so called because there is no sea in sight, and Russell Street in Stroud is a tribute to Lord John Russell, a former local MP who was prime minister twice.

COTSWOLD RHYMING SLANG

Now that you have learned more about the stories behind Gloucestershire place names, it is time to learn some Gloucestershire rhyming slang. I have always wanted to create our own version to give the Cockneys a run for their money and my brilliant radio listeners came up trumps by helping me to come up with the following:

'Could you lend me an Edward because I'm off to do a bit of Jonny Coppin?'
   'It's a bit Stow today.'
   'The weather is a bit Moreton.'
   'Just before I go I'll just have a quick Laurie.'

Got it? Edward Jenner = tenner; Johnny Coppin (folk singer) = shopping; Stow-on-the-Wold = cold; Moreton-in-Marsh = harsh; Laurie Lee = pee, so Jimmy Riddle can now retire!

'Just had a lovely chat with the Severn bore, I bought her some Gloucester Docks and a bunch of Guitings and some glue for her Bishop's Cleeve. She said you've got some Coaley, talking about my hair like that.'

Severn bore = mother-in-law; Gloucester Docks = socks; Guiting Power = flower and Bishop's Cleeve = weave (much better than 'syrup of figs' for wig); Coaley Peak = cheek.

'Head's feeling a bit Awre. Had one too many Duntisbournes last night, need some Steam Mills.'

Awre = sore; Duntisbourne Leer = beer and Steam Mills = pills.

Rather than phrases, here are some stand-alone examples:

Cherry and whites = tights
Gloucestershire's classic version of a lardy treat, Dripper = nipper
Lower Slaughter = daughter

May Hill = ill
Cliffords Mesne = keen
Staunton and Corse = hoarse
Westonbirt = shirt

And finally, 'I really need a Hetty Pegler's.' I won't explain that one.

MATCH THE ADJECTIVES IN THE CLAMOUR FOR THE COTSWOLD BRAND

Travelling around the county, you may have spotted how some towns have changed their names in an attempt to attract more visitors. Can you tell me which places use the following titles?

Queen of the Cotswolds
Capital of the Cotswolds
Centre for the Cotswolds
Venice of the Cotswolds
Gateway to the Cotswolds

The undisputed Queen can be found nestling just north of Stroud, the stunning small town of Painswick. I have never found out when Painswick assumed this title but it is fully deserved with its classic Cotswold stone buildings, the prettiest churchyard you will ever see and a history of weaving and woollen mills.

Cirencester has always been accredited with the undisputed branding of Capital of the Cotswolds. It makes sense on a geographical and administrative level and for its sheer size, energy and history.

If you drive into Cheltenham you will see many signs with the logo 'Centre for the Cotswolds'. This is a clever line as they don't claim to be the centre *of* the Cotswolds. They simply offer a perfect place to base yourselves for the duration of your visit.

I love the fact that the dreamy River Windrush trickling under those stunning low Cotswold bridges in Bourton-on-the-Water has led, quite rightly, to the title Venice of the Cotswolds. It is simple, clever and paints an iconic picture.

The Venice of the Cotswolds, Bourton-on-the-Water.

The final one is the most controversial. Where has the prime claim to being the Gateway to the Cotswolds? A quick internet search reveals that Burford uses this title the most, followed by Farringdon. Considering that you can enter the Cotswolds from any direction, any of the following (and more) could claim it: Cinderford, Bath, Malvern, Warwick, Birmingham, Scunthorpe.

TWEE TOUR

If you have already been to the Queen, the Capital, the Centre, the Venice and the Gateway and fancy going further afield on a 'Twee Tour' of Gloucestershire, I would be delighted to take you. Estate agents always claim a romantic address increases the value of a house, so why not allow me to try and sell you a property in Glorious Gloucestershire? How about buying a little cottage in the hamlet of Cockadilly near the sweetest village of Nympsfield? If you fancy being upwardly mobile you could splash the cash in Upper Up in South Cerney, where you could also purchase a des res for your pooches in Bow Wow. If you have an adventurous spirit you could move to North Pole Lane near Gorsley, or if you prefer the quiet

145

life, the elusive Land of Nod in the Forest of Dean could be for you, if you can find it! Many of my Forest friends know of such a place, but not one can place it on a map! Fans of *Carry On* movies might like an assortment of bottoms including Nanny Farmer's, Tomtits, Frog Trotters, Waterley, Green and Nettleton. Those of you not worried about the health police and cholesterol issues might like to invest in something picturesque on Buttermilk Lane. Finally, can I tempt you with Strawberry Hill (a vineyard) near Newent, Ready Penny, Paradise on the A46 or The Heavens, which is a place just above Brimscombe and Thrupp?

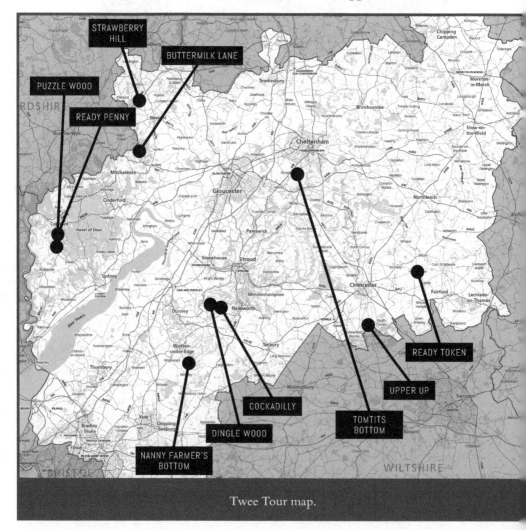

Twee Tour map.

LOCAL PLACE NAMES EXPLAINED

Hopefully you have already stored away all sorts of information that will give you a head start in any local quiz. In case you need to know the meanings of some of our place names, here is a selection.

Gloucester: The Welsh name for the city was Caerloyw, the second half of which was pronounced 'gloyw', meaning 'bright'. The Old English 'cester' came from the Roman for a fort or walled city. So, Gloucester means the bright place/fort/walled city. The spelling 'Gloster' was used by the Gloster Aircraft Company because the Americans couldn't pronounce it when it was spelled 'Gloucester'.

Cheltenham: People often think Cheltenham is related to the River Chelt. This is not the case. The River Chelt was originally referred to as the Alr. The Chelt bit of the town's name is thought to have originated in Saxon times from a man named Celta, who was an influential figure in the area.

Cinderford: This is a logical one. The derivation of Old English 'sinder-ford' is linked to the iron smelting that went on in the town, leaving deposits of cinders.

Clapham: This area of Gloucester is very near to Kingsholm rugby stadium and my 'source' was born there. He is my only source, I love him dearly and he swears the following is true but you can take it with a pinch of salt if you like. My mate, Maurice, remembers the 1940s when many people in the area had pigeons and after a long, tiring race people would stand outside and cheer them back to their owners. They would 'clap 'em' back home.

Cotswold: Simply 'cots', meaning sheep enclosure, and 'wold', meaning gentle hill. Put them together and bingo.

Lydney: This derives from the Old English word 'lida-eg' or 'lydan-eg'. However, some claim it means the island of the sailor.

Paradise: Paradise is just off the A46 near Painswick but where did the name come from? The most popular explanation links to Charles I, who was fed up that the folk of Gloucester had held off his army and needed cheering up. He could see things unfolding from Painswick Beacon, so he turned the other way and, seeing the little hamlet below, said something along the lines of 'this is truly paradise'.

Redmarley D'Abitot: This is one of the more mysterious and enchanting names in the county. Redmarley derives from Old English words 'hreod' and 'leah', and is thought to mean either a woodland clearing with a reedy pond or a border. The D'Abitot part refers to a family who were Norman lords of the manor and were referred to in the Doomsday Book.

Stonehouse: This is another simple one coming from the Old English 'stan-hus', which refers to a house built of stone.

Stroud: The name derives from the Old English word 'strod' and means marshy ground.

Tewkesbury: The general consensus is that the name originates from an earlier name of theocsbury or teodekesberie. Theoc or Teodec was the name of a Saxon hermit who came to the area in the seventh century.

Woodmancote: There are three of these in the county, located near Bishop's Cleeve, Rendcomb and Dursley. It describes a place where a woodman had a cottage.

Upper and Lower Slaughter: The word Slaughter does not suggest anything sinister, although some have wondered if it refers to a bloody battle or a grisly local murder. It simply means the muddy place.

Lower Slaughter. (Cotswolds Tourism, Cotswolds.com)

The county is scattered with places with 'ham' and 'ton', which both simply mean homestead or farm settlement.

Rivers often find their way into place names. The geographical position of the River Leach explains Northleach and Eastleach. The same river discharges into the Thames near Lechlade and Lech is a corruption of Leach.

North and South Cerney are far apart but share the River Churn in common, hence Chur and Cern.

Combe means valley, as in Winchcombe, Pitchcombe and Rendcombe.

Fords, as in a well or spring, are referred to in the names Fairford, Kempsford and Ford.

The Forest of Dean has many wonderful place names, including onomatopoeic The Pludds. This hamlet near Ruardean derives from the Middle English word 'pludde', meaning a pool or puddle.

Strip-and-at-it is a fantastic name and can be found in the heart of the Forest of Dean. The simple explanation for this saucy place is that it used to be a colliery that closed in 1925.

We have three Golden Valleys in the county. Let's start with the A40, that big lump of tarmac that straddles the M5 between Cheltenham and Gloucester. Before the Golden Valley Bypass was built that whole area of pasture land was known as the Golden 'Vale', not 'Valley', and the person who owns the naming rights to this area is reputed to be Sir Walter Raleigh. According to my local history society sources, he was taking a stroll up Leckhampton Hill gazing out over the fields looking towards the Forest of Dean and he proclaimed it as a golden vale.

The Chalford Valley heading out of Stroud towards Cirencester and Kemble is our second Golden Valley and it is most often attributed to a comment made by Queen Victoria from her carriage on her way through the county. Others suggest it has more to do with the rich woollen cloth heritage that certainly made many people wealthy in former days. Whatever view you take, it is a breathtaking stretch of land full of golden views, hidden secrets and magical walks. To squeeze every drop out of this particular valley, I recommend one of my favourite bike rides from Sapperton to Frampton Mansell, then down to Chalford. It is heavenly.

The derivation of our final Golden Valley has always eluded me but I recommend a visit to the gorgeous gully of gold situated between Ruardean and Drybrook in the Forest of Dean.

LOCAL PRONUNCIATIONS

Having hosted radio shows across Gloucestershire for thirty years, there is one local pronunciation that still haunts me to this day. The Over/Ooover debate will be raging long after I am dead and gone and it would be more than my life is worth to commit in print which version I think is correct.

Over is just outside Gloucester on the A40 as you head towards the city from Highnam. It is famous for its fabulous Over Farm Market, Over bridge and its capacity to cause huge rows. It was first recorded in 1005 as 'Ofre', which comes from the Old English 'ofer', indicating it was the place at the ridge or the slope. Whichever way you choose to pronounce it there will be a vociferous reaction the other way. Trust me, I was pinned to a wall by a local WI member once when she thought I was in favour of Ooover.

Other pronunciations to watch out for include: Ampney, as in Down Ampney, Ampney Crucis, Ampney St Mary all have a silent 'p', so the correct pronunciation is 'Amknee'. Southrop is 'Suth-Rup' not 'South-Rop'. In the Forest of Dean, Cliffords Mesne is pronounced Cliffords 'Mean'. Michaelwood Services on the M5 should be pronounced 'Mikkel' Wood as it is named after the ancient woodland it is built around. If you are born in Tewkesbury, it will always be pronounced 'Chucksbury'. There is an older generation that have always pronounced Prinknash as it is spelled but over the years it has morphed into 'prinish'. I am staying out of it. I am not staying out of this one though: there is no THE in Moreton-in-Marsh but so many people pop one in and it drives me crazy. I know it shouldn't. I know there is more to life but it drives me mad. There is, however a THE in Bourton-on-the-Water but some people leave it out. Probably the people who put it back into Moreton.

LOCAL NICKNAMES

Here's a list of some Gloucestershire place names that have been changed slightly by locals or rivals from elsewhere in the county.

Longlevens is known as 'Short twelves'; Broadwell as 'Bradall'; Evenlode as 'Emlod'; Broadway as 'Broddie'; Chipping Campden just as 'Campden'; Conndicot as 'the Docks'; and Charlton Kings as 'Yarley' (no one knows why). People from Stroud refer to Dursley as 'Drizzly' and in Gloucester, Hucclecote is nicknamed 'Chucklecote', while Abbeymead is sometimes referred to as 'Shabbymead'. North Cotswold folk often call Snowshill 'Snozzle' and locals in Upton St Leonards often refer to it as 'Upton St rain hard'. Nibley monument is affectionately known as 'Nobbly Minument'.

Nibley Monument or
Nobbly Minument.

In the Stroud valleys the beautiful village of Chalford stretches up the hillside and the term 'Neddyshire' was coined when deliveries were made by donkeys up the steep, narrow lanes.

Finally, Oakridge on the tops above Stroud is a wonderful place for a bracing walk with amazing views and it is known locally as 'little Russia' or 'little Siberia'. It can be a bit chilly and isolated up there but it is well worth a visit.

ALGERNON TOADSMORE STRIKES AGAIN

Dame Jilly Cooper uses towns and villages as inspiration for her characters' names to avoid accidentally naming a real person. My audience helped me compile a list of characters she could use in future novels derived from Gloucestershire place names. These are the ones Dame Jilly loved the most when I took my humble cast list to her: Arthur Winchcombe, the grumpy landlord; Dixie Dumbleton, the village flirt; Hester Sway, the glamorous health food shop owner; Dr James Slimbridge, the slightly sinister GP; Cordelia Wyck-Rissington, the extremely efficient secretary of the local WI; Bartholomew Cockadilly, the crusty former local newspaper editor; and Algernon Toadsmore, the slightly shifty verger at Gloucester Cathedral.

How to Squeeze Every Drop Out of Glorious Gloucestershire's Name Game

The first thing to do is with all this information is to plan a strategic road trip with friends so that you can show off your local knowledge for all it is worth. I suggest you head to Painswick Beacon for the incredible view and tell the story about Charles I. If you can cope with confined spaces, a visit to Hetty Pegler's Tump is a joy but wear old clothes and take a torch with you. Spend some time in Cranham and search out Gladys' Leap with your OS coordinates or Google Maps.

Visit Snowshill Manor in early July when you can also stroll through the fields of lavender. Most importantly, use the word Snozzle in the company of an elderly local and you will make a friend for life. Finally, if you are feeling brave, choose one pronunciation of Over or Ooover, go into the Over Farm Market shop and café and repeat your choice of pronunciation as loudly and as often as you can. I suggest you wear a speedy pair of running shoes just in case.

CUMMINGS' COUNTY QUIZ

ROUND EIGHT

1. True or false? The Cotswold Motoring Museum and Toy Collection in Bourton-on-the-Water announced a new collection in 2005. As part of their publicity campaign they hired a Gloucester rugby star for the press launch. Recent signing Mike Tindall cut the ribbon but hilariously then got stuck when he squeezed himself into the vintage little yellow TV car character Brum. As the cameras rolled it took precisely four minutes to extricate him.

2. Which famous Forest of Dean playwright wrote *Pennies from Heaven* and *The Singing Detective*?

3. Is Hagloe Crab a native apple, pear or sheep?

4. Which famous Gloucester school was once based on Eastgate Street and Barton Street?

5. Complete the phrase 'Stow-on-the-Wold where the wind ...'?

6. Which motorway takes you over the Severn Bridge?

7. What year was Gloucester Rugby Club formed?

8. Where in the county has been dubbed 'Covent Garden of the Cotswolds' and 'Notting Hill with Wellies'?

9. What famous place in the Cotswolds was discovered by a group of men digging to retrieve a ferret down a rabbit hole?

10. Prorsum Semper is our county's motto and features on our coat of arms. What does it mean?

12

CHERRY AND WHITE HEAVEN

TO TRULY EXPERIENCE everything Gloucestershire has to offer, you must, at least once in your life, go to a rugby game at Kingsholm Stadium. For many I will be preaching to the converted but even for diehard Cherry and White fans I dare you to read the next few words without 'welling up'. To convey the depth of connection the club has within the community, I need to share a snapshot of a speech I gave recently in front of players, coaches and friends at Kingsholm.

During my final week hosting the BBC Radio Gloucestershire breakfast show the club very kindly gave me a really special send-off. They knew how much the club means to me and arranged an evening in the Legends' Lounge bar where we could enjoy Gloucester Brewery ale, some delicious food and the company of current club staff including coach George Skivington, captain Lewis Ludlow and former player Alex Brown. In front of sixty friends and family the overriding theme of my speech was about how far the tentacles of the club reach into your life in a deep and emotional way.

On the day my dad died, 28 December 2017, I drove up to Yorkshire in a daze. On the way back on 30 December, my wife, Jo, texted me and said, 'Call in on your other family on the way home.' Still in a muddle, I didn't know what she meant. Then the penny dropped. In the mayhem I had forgotten that Gloucester had a home game against Sale that afternoon. I squeezed myself into the caring huddle of friends in a sold-out Shed and watched us win 20–16.

In the Shed at Kingsholm with Maurice.

The Shed is a very special place. The friends I stand with are like another family full of fun, warmth and mickey taking. The place where I stand every match has an even deeper connection with me after I snuggled down in a sleeping bag one cold October night drifting in and out of light, restless sleep in the place I love so much. I have spent two nights sleeping on the concrete where I usually stand to raise awareness for local homeless charities. The legendary banter in the Shed is epitomised by my special friend Maurice Blakeway, who has been watching Gloucester rugby since 1946. I won't repeat some of the comments he makes to opposition players, the touch judge or the referee, but I can tell you they have provided hilarity for 'Shed Heads' for more than sixty years. Many years ago, he took a whistle into the Shed and during a game gave a it a good old blast. On hearing the whistle, the players all stopped and waited for the referee's decision, which never came. Maurice always has a supply of rum with him but tradition states that we are not allowed any until the first frost of the year. My kind if deceitful radio listeners would send me photos of minus temperatures and frosty lawns in early September to allow us to have a tot at the beginning of the season.

I also mentioned in my speech the thrill of taking my daughters to their first game, the post-match buzz in the city after a win, the memories of thrashing Bath 64–0 and seeing grown men cry on the way out, turning Reading Services Cherry and White on the way home from London having won the European Challenge Cup at The Stoop, James Hook's last-minute monster kick to beat Sarries when we all thought we had lost, and bumping into a fellow Gloucester fan who spotted my Cherry and White shirt in a street market in Buenos Aires.

I started supporting the club in the early 1990s. Imagine what a treasure trove of memories fans who have supported them for much longer must have. I love the buzz of turning the corner and walking out onto the Kingsholm Road with the heady hit of the smell of chips, vinegar, fried onions and Gloucester Old Spot sausage as you approach the ground. The beers before and after the game and sharing anticipation, hope, despair and exhilaration with fellow fans are also an essential part of the experience.

Family fun in the Shed.

There are many brilliant books about the history and statistics of the club but my mission in this chapter is to do something a little different. I want to share how it 'feels' to be part of the club and I urge you to sample the atmosphere just once, either on a typical Saturday afternoon or when there is an intoxicating vibe under the lights on a Friday evening. Having decided to leave my broadcasting career to concentrate on writing, I knew what my last words on the radio would be. They were simply, 'I'll see you in the Shed.' Here's a deal – if you find me in the Shed I will find you a tot of rum as long as you help me confiscate Maurice's whistle.

13

ROYAL GLOUCESTERSHIRE

CAST YOUR MIND back to the sombre period between the death of Queen Elizabeth II and her funeral. A stoic, tired, emotionally drained King Charles visited each of the four nations. During that unforgettable time, we were reviewing news stories for the next day's show when something jumped out at me. King Charles was going to break his tour with a night's rest at Highgrove. A lot had been mentioned about his love of this iconic Georgian house and whether he would still use it. I knew immediately what our headline would be and where we needed to host the show from. The new king was going to be waking up in his beloved house in his beloved county. Many felt chuffed and proud that during one of the most tumultuous times of his life, he wanted to be here. The house used to belong to Maurice Macmillan, son of the former Prime Minister Harold Macmillan. Various sources suggest a figure of between £800,000 to £1 million was paid to secure the property in 1980 by the Duchy of Cornwall. When Prince and Princess Michael of Kent lived at Nether Lypiatt Manor near Stroud, Highgrove used to form part of 'the Royal Triangle', with Princess Anne down the road at the Gatcombe Park Estate along with her daughter Zara and son-in-law Mike Tindall making up the third point on the royal Gloucestershire map.

I have lived close to Tetbury since the early 1990s and I have picked up many royal anecdotes from the locals. William and Harry's favourite pubs for a wild night out included the Rattlebone in Sherston, the Cat and Custard Pot in Shipton Moyne and the Vine Tree in Norton, which is the location Harry alludes in his book *Spare*. We won't go into details as to what happened in the nearby fields. The last time I had a pint in the

Tetbury Market House at Christmas, where Queen Camilla switched on the lights. (Cotswolds Tourism, Cotswolds.com)

beer garden at the Cat and Custard Pot, the 2nd Earl of Snowdon was at the next table downing a pint. Also referred to as Viscount Linley, he is the only son of Princess Margaret and Antony Armstrong-Jones. I knew the owner of Cotswold Costumes in Nailsworth, the shop where Harry made that injudicious choice of partywear and it became the talk of the town for months. I once nearly ran over the boys' nanny, Tiggy Legge-Bourke, when she stepped off the pavement in Tetbury without looking.

I will finish on my favourite tenuous brush with royalty, which involves the honour of switching on the Christmas lights in Tetbury. The iconic market house in Tetbury looked stunning with its dreamy string of golden lights draped beautifully around the walls. My only problem when pushing the plunger was to not be daunted by the couple who had done it the year before ... the future king and queen. According to my Tetbury 'Snout', Camilla was keen to work out how the plunger connected to the electrics and kept asking for clarification. The plunger is fake and it is Sid in a little room underneath the building who flicks the switch. As the clock was ticking to showtime she was still debating the technical details when an exasperated organiser said, 'Just push the bloody plunger!'

How to Squeeze Every Drop of Royal Blood Out of Glorious Regal Gloucestershire

If you love our historical royal connections, visit Berkeley Castle (where Edward II died), Gloucester Cathedral (where Edward II is buried), the Speech House in the Forest of Dean (a hunting lodge built for King Charles II in 1669), Sudeley Castle (where the only queen to be laid to rest on private land, Katherine Parr, is buried), the New Inn in Gloucester (Lady Jane Grey was proclaimed Queen of England on the first-floor gallery after the death of King Edward VI) and the Pittville Pump Rooms in Cheltenham (King George III came to the town to take the healing spa waters). Book a ticket for the Cheltenham Festival on the day of the Queen Mother Champion Chase. The late Queen Mother adored the festival and on her way to the course would always pop into the Prestbury village store to pick up her favourite chocolates.

Explore Tetbury and have a look in the Highgrove shop. One local told me he had heard an American tourist declare, 'Oh my God, the king lives above that little shop!'

Highgrove Shop in Tetbury.
(Cotswolds Tourism, Cotswolds.com)

Down the road is Westonbirt Arboretum, the king's next-door garden. Local rumour has it that it would sometimes open privately early in the morning for the then Prince of Wales to enjoy an undisturbed stroll. I am not convinced but it is a popular local belief.

And finally, enjoy a different view of Highgrove from one of my treasured cycle routes. This can be a gentle walk or ride along a dreamy lane taking you for a secret glimpse of the back of the house. Find the Hare and Hounds Hotel on the A433 from Tetbury, turn right up Bowldown Road, then right along Hookshouse Lane. Through the fields on your right you'll have that unique view of Highgrove.

CUMMINGS' COUNTY QUIZ

ROUND NINE

1. True or false? Here is a little twist to our ice cream heritage. Bond legend Roger Moore rang the boss of Wall's and suggested they come up with a chocolate-covered ice cream and put it on a stick. This was the origin of the Magnum we know and love today.

2. Who was the Ethiopian emperor who visited Cheltenham in 1937 taking in the Ladies' College, the Pump Rooms and the Lido with lunch at the Queens Hotel?

3. Which of the following doesn't have a disused airfield: Chedworth, Bibury or Frampton on Severn?

4. What does SARA stand for?

5. Where did Mike and Zara live before moving to the Gatcombe Estate?

6. Which river runs through Bourton-on-the-Water?

7. In which sport was Fred Archer a local legend?

8. Frost, Thomas and Abercrombie were known collectively as the Dymock what?

9. Where would you find a Gloucester rugby player, a cheese roller, a Cheltenham jockey and a Forest of Dean miner all looking down on you from on high?

10. What type of swans do we love watching return to Slimbridge in the autumn?

14

THE GLORIOUS GLOSTERS

I COULDN'T POSSIBLY write a book called *Glorious Gloucestershire* without mentioning a group of people who evoke an astonishing amount of pride, passion and admiration. I was in no doubt about the strength of feeling towards the Glorious Glosters when my radio show phone lines went into meltdown at the time when the iconic 'Back Badge' came under threat. Unique to the British Army, the Glosters wore badges on the front and rear of their berets. The honour was bestowed to recognise their heroics against Napoleon's army in Alexandria, Egypt, in 1801. The badge survived the merger of the Royal Gloucestershire, Berkshire and Wiltshire regiments in 1994, but pressure grew to remove it when a second merger was planned. A fierce campaign was launched because it meant so much to generations of people in the county with ties to the regiment. In forty years on the radio I have never witnessed such a reaction. In the end it was agreed the badge would be worn on the ceremonial dress of the newly formed Rifles Regiment.

The Glosters are most famous for the Battle of Imjin River in April 1951. In a huge turning point in the Korean War, 700 Glosters held out against more than 10,000 Chinese troops and famously fought a last stand on Hill 235. Over the years when veterans have returned for a remembrance ceremony they are treated like royalty. Hill 235, where the Glorious Glosters were famously ordered to 'Hold on where you are', is now known as Gloster Hill.

To meet and chat to one of these veterans is a real honour and I have had the delight of spending time with the legendary Tommy Clough. Tommy was a former prisoner of war who served as a gunner in the

Jack Russell's painting of Glorious
Gloster veteran Tommy Clough.

Battle of Imjin River. He is a charismatic gent who has told me snippets
of his story on many occasions. Thanks to former England cricketer
and artist Jack Russell, I now know even more about Tommy and his
comrades' experiences. Jack made it his mission to track down and paint
as many of the surviving Glosters as he could. During these sittings,
many veterans opened up and shared stories that had been locked away
for many years. Jack told me how his fascination with this regiment
started with a chance meeting with a man in the Prince Albert pub in
Rodborough. Jack takes up the story:

> His name was Henry Pegler, and he was badly wounded at the Battle
> of Imjin River. He used to sit in the corner of the Albert sipping away
> all night at his gin. I asked the landlord Richard Johnson one night
> why I had never seen him eat anything from the bar menu, and he said
> he was prisoner of war with the Chinese for two years and his stomach
> had shrunk so he didn't eat much. He also said not to disturb him.

One evening I plucked up the courage to ask him if he would teach me to drive because he was an official driving instructor. And he was great once you got to know him! He did well to get me through my test because I paid more attention to what he used to tell me about the battle. He never talked about the prisoner-of-war camps though – I've learned more about that doing the portraits.

Jack's former team, Gloucestershire County Cricket Club, was approached during the merger issues to see if it would be interested in preserving the tradition of the Back Badge in its own club caps. GCCC happily accepted the honour of keeping the tradition alive. The Back Badge was first worn at the Cheltenham Cricket Festival in 2006 and whenever Gloucestershire wins a game, the old Glosters regimental 'victory song' is belted out by the players.

We are the Glosters famed for our attack …
When we have served our country and answered the trumpet call
Take us back to Gloucestershire, most glorious land of all.

How to Squeeze Every Drop Out of Glorious Gloucestershire's Military Heritage

A visit to the Soldiers of Gloucestershire Museum at Gloucester Docks is a must. *The Final Roll Call* by Jack Russell MBE and Matthew A. Holden is a brilliant read and all proceeds go to the museum.

15

DID YOU KNOW?

THIS COUNTY IS chock-a-block with an array of barely believable facts. I would like to arm you with a few gems to be dropped into conversations when you feel the need to shock, surprise, educate or simply show off. Enjoy the following selection box of tasty Gloucestershire goodies.

SIR PETER SCOTT GOES TO NEVERLAND

Did you know the following facts about Sir Peter Scott, founder of the Wildfowl and Wetlands Centre at Slimbridge, who is known as the Father of Conservation?

He was named after Peter Pan and author J.M. Barrie was his godfather.

He was the only child of the explorer Captain Scott (Scott of the Antarctic), who famously instructed his wife to 'make the boy interested in natural history'.

He was a famous broadcaster and commentated on the Coronation of Queen Elizabeth II. He presented many radio programmes, including *Nature Parliament* in the 1940s, and a BBC nature television programme live from his house at Slimbridge.

He invented a harness used by racing crews to hang from a sailing boat, now known as a trapeze. He also helped design the camouflage used by British Second World War warships.

He founded the Society of Wildlife Artists and is best known for his paintings of flocks of geese, ducks and other wading birds.

He was the first person to be knighted for services to conservation, in 1973. As well as being a founder of WWT and WWF, he drew their respective swan and panda logos.

He won a bronze Olympic medal in 1936 for sailing. He was also a British glider pilot champion and a national championship-standard ice skater.

EDWARD JENNER AND THE AIR BALLOON

The now demolished but never forgotten pub the Air Balloon is said to be named after the landing of a hydrogen balloon launched by Edward Jenner. The pub near Birdlip was originally called the New Inn and there is a theory that Jenner's own aerial adventures led to the name being changed. He launched a hydrogen balloon, which was probably one of the UK's earliest such flights, from the courtyard at Berkeley Castle on 2 September 1748 and it landed at Kingscote. It is claimed that Jenner then relaunched the balloon, which drifted another 14 miles to the Cotswold Escarpment near Birdlip. The pub was renamed the Balloon Inn and then became the Air Balloon in 1796.

READY FOR TAKE-OFF ON THE M5

Adjoining the Brockworth airfield where the first jet flight took place was another airfield, RAF Moreton Valence. During the Second World War, the Armstrong Whitworth Albemarle bomber was trialled there and it was also used by the Gloster Aircraft Company to test the Meteor and Javelin fighter aircraft. The airfield closed in 1962, and when the M5 was built a few years later they apparently used some of the footings of the old Moreton Valence runway. When you are driving south down the M5 between junctions 12 and 13 there is a stretch of motorway that is dead straight and it is here that you are said to be driving on the old runway.

THE EXACT CENTRE OF GLORIOUS GLOUCESTERSHIRE

Do you know where the precise middle of Gloucestershire is? As part of my radio show, we asked Ordnance Survey to do some calculations and they came up with Moorfield Road in Brockworth on the outskirts of Gloucester. If you take the district of the Forest of Dean and apply their computer calculations you will also be able to discover the location of the geographical heart of the forest. Many people think the Speech House or Parkend represent the true centre of the Forest, but the official 'middle bit' is somewhere between Blaize Bailey and Blaize Bailey Farm.

FERN TICKET

Did you know about the most prized possession in the Forest of Dean? The stories behind the powers and significance of owning a Fern Ticket are many and varied. It is claimed that having your first amorous experience in the woods entitles you to a 'Fern Ticket'. Others suggest that owning one gives you certain entitlement to a little al fresco slap and tickle. The following is printed on the ticket:

My treasured possession.

Have you ever made love in a bed of fern?
Then, alas, my friend you've a lot to learn!

All I will say is, my lovely friends in the Forest keep sending me them and I am not going to reveal in print if I have ever made use of one.

DAVID AND GOLIATH

The Uley Brewery once produced a special one-off beer for the Frocester Beer Festival called Oil of Uley. The manufactures of Oil of Ulay/ Olay were not happy and their legal department sent the late great Chas Wright and his team at the brewery a legal letter. I will never forget the fun we had in the media stirring up a storm of indignation and incredulity. Any threat of legal action was soon withdrawn.

HOW MUCH IS THE CHELTENHAM GOLD CUP TROPHY WORTH?

The actual Cheltenham Gold Cup trophy reportedly consists of 644g, or approximately 1lb 7oz, of nine-carat gold. According to cheltenham-festivalblog.co.uk, this makes the trophy worth over £7,000. *Horse and Hounds* magazine places its worth a little higher at £10,000.

SPACE SHUTTLE EMERGENCY LANDING SITE

RAF Fairford was designated as a possible landing site in the event of something going wrong when the Space Shuttle was in operation. A team of NASA experts were always on hand just in case the Shuttle crew had to abort the mission after take-off. The 2-mile-long runway at Fairford was the UK's only Transoceanic Abort Landing site for the Shuttle, and one of only four in western Europe.

Sandford Parks Lido, Cheltenham. (David Hanks)

SWIMMING WITH THE STARS

Boxing champs Joe Louis and Johnny 'Tarzan' Weissmuller made a public appearance at Sandford Parks Lido in Cheltenham. How do I know this? The late, great Ron Coltman told me. Ron was Mr Lido. He loved the place and worked there for many years. The stars were entertaining members of the American forces who were stationed in the town prior to the D-Day assault on the Normandy beaches. Ron told me with great pride that Olympic Gold medal swimmer Weissmuller dived off the top board, swam 50m under water, and was hauled out by Louis.

NO 'ELEVENSES' IN LITTLEDEAN

You can't take a short break for a snack and cup of tea at 11 a.m. in Littledean because it is never eleven o'clock there. The clock on the tower of St Ethelbert's Church has the wrong Roman numeral. Instead of XI for 11 it actually has IX, which is 9.

GLOUCESTERSHIRE IN NUMBERS

I love a juicy number. Sometimes it reveals something you didn't know, sometimes it shocks you, and sometimes it is simply mildly interesting. See what you make of these: 390 churches, 1 naturist society, 4 motorways, 23 A roads, 3,058 commercial farm holdings, 361 villages, 46 trig points, 600 stone stiles and 500 Downton lorries. I would never have guessed there were 500 Downton lorries. This iconic haulage company is based on the A38 south of Gloucester and when we see one of their purple trucks a long way from home it gives many of us a lovely warm feeling. The four motorways are the M5, M48, M50 and M96 at Moreton Fire College. The M4 is South Gloucestershire, not Gloucestershire. And finally, we have, of course, 4,000 miles of drystone walls across the Cotswolds.

THE LONGEST WHAT IN THE COUNTRY?

It stretches for 2,640ft, provides a venue for gastronomic gluttony, classic English summer sports, sheep racing and has a choice of a pub at either end. I am alluding to the magnificent green at Frampton on Severn, which is the longest village green in the country. The green is known as Rosamund's Green after Henry II's mistress, Rosamund Clifford, a member of the family closely associated with Frampton from the eleventh century. I have heard stories of elver eating competitions and the Frampton Feast, which back in the day included huge amounts of food, cider and bare-knuckle boxing. You can also see sheep racing on the green and that wonderful sight in the summer of a quintessential game of cricket. I had always dreamed of playing in one of these games and the dream came true when Frampton agreed to a charity match with BBC Radio Gloucestershire. While fielding at slip I broke a rib with a rather clumsy dive but manfully opened the batting a few minutes later. This might explain my shameful three-ball duck. A couple of months later I was back falling off an electric scooter while filming for BBC *Points West*. A year later I ended up in Tetbury Hospital after tearing my calf at Frampton tennis club just off the green. Despite all this I absolutely love the place.

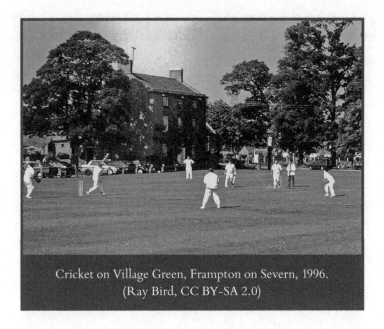

Cricket on Village Green, Frampton on Severn, 1996.
(Ray Bird, CC BY-SA 2.0)

THE FOLLOWING MIGHT NOT BE TRUE

Did you hear the one about a swimming pool on the top of the Eagle Tower building? How about the iconic Verve album cover featuring May Hill? Maybe I could tempt you with a tale about how Café René in Gloucester was inspired by the BBC sitcom *'Allo 'Allo*. All these stories have been told many times and over the years the folklore, for some, has become fact. When Eagle Tower was constructed in the late 1960s, rumour had it that they had snuck in a swimming pool on the roof, but this is a complete lie. Richard Ashcroft from The Verve has a place at the foot of May Hill at Taynton, but the tree-clad image of the band on their classic *Urban Hymns* album was not from our wonderful landmark. Café René was inspired by French philosopher René Descartes. Finally, is there a café on the top of May Hill? A supremely talented local broadcaster insisted for years that there was. It is worth a trip to the top of this mesmerising hill to check it out.

CUMMINGS' COUNTY QUIZ

ROUND TEN

1. True or false? I was responsible for losing Dame Jilly Cooper's faithful rescue greyhound Bluebell. We went for a walk with my two rescue lurchers in the woods near her Bisley home and my two naughty scruffs led Bluebell astray. I eventually found the three escapees in Oakridge Lynch.

2. Why was the Cheltenham Festival called off in March 2001?

3. In which part of Gloucestershire would you find the Scowles, Mork and Netherend?

4. Why is 1643 such a meaningful date for people in Gloucester?

5. Is Broadway Tower in or out of Gloucestershire?

6. We have two places called Nags Head, one near Avening and one in the Forest of Dean. What purpose do they serve?

7. What is the link between the Forest of Dean and the Spanish Armada?

8. Which local theatre is very unpopular with pigs?

9. The Snooty Fox pub in Tetbury used to have a large upstairs ballroom, but which local high society people used to dance there?

10. What is the answer to this cryptic clue to somewhere in the county: 'Embarrassed Reggae Legend'?

'TWAS THE NIGHT BEFORE CHRISTMAS – THE GLOUCESTERSHIRE VERSION

I WROTE THIS with apologies to Clement Clarke Moore in 2007 and I am delighted that it has become a much-loved part of Christmas for so many people. It has been read in abbeys, cathedrals and churches across the county and heard online as well as on the radio. I am also told readings are shared among friends and family on Christmas Eve.

'Twas was the night before Christmas when all through the Shire,
Men from the Cotswolds were caught in the mire.
With their shopping not done on the day from hell,
They usher up help from Esso and Shell.
At the window small faces were pressed to the sill,
But Daddy was stuck back on Crickley Hill.
The children were ushered to snuggle in bed,
While visions of iPhones danced in their head.
Then all of a sudden they heard such a clatter,
Daddy was back but what was the matter?
He threw down his car keys and furrowed his brow,
Then turned to Mama and started a row.
'Why leave things so late?' she exclaimed with a sigh,
'It's just what men do, there's no reason why!'
As the magic of Christmas was beginning to go,

They re-lit their fire 'neath the mistletoe.
As the snow iced the land like a white Cotswold cake,
The sound of St Nick was beginning to break,
When what to their wondering eyes should appear,
A miniature sleigh with eight small reindeer.
This jolly old man with his bundles of toys,
Looked down from on high at our girls and boys.
He appeared in the sky as if sent from heaven,
Flew over the Forest and followed the Severn.
To the old bridge he soared then shouted out loud,
Come Donder and Blitzen we're going to Stroud.
He swept up the valley where the mills once stood,
Then made to refuel at the Enchanted Wood.
Highgrove was quiet as he spotted the trees,
A runway of lights made the landing a breeze.
The pies and the carrots as always were laid,
In a neat little pile by the Acer Glade.
With a nod to dear Rudolph and a tug on the rein,
Said bye to Westonbirt and got going again.
Up through the branches they rose higher and higher,
And headed for Gloucester and the midnight choir.
The cathedral they spied in the blink of an eye,
The echoes of carols rose up in the sky.
And then with a twinkling, mischievous grin,
St Nick took his team for their favourite spin.
From Robinswood Hill they revved up the pace,
Time now for fun at that prized landing space.
With a weave and a whoosh and sleigh full of hope,
What fun they all had at Matson ski slope.
Now off to the Cotswolds to deliver more bounty,
A dry-stone wall map led them over the county.
From Birdlip to Bisley from Moreton to Stow,
The work kept on going down the chimneys below.
With his job nearly done in the Cotswolds that night,
That jolly old elf made one last flight.
The final location for them to deliver,
Had its own mini village and a tree in the river.

The children in Bourton, they lay sound asleep,
Of St Nick and Rudolph they heard not a peep.
But one little boy heard the tinkling of ash,
So away to his window he flew like a flash.
And then to his joy at this late hour,
Spied a tiny old sleigh over Broadway Tower.
He waved as the reindeer flew further away,
What joys they'd left him for Christmas Day.
Then as if by magic he thought he could see,
St Nick in the moonlight smiling at 'me'.
He heard him exclaim as he drove out of sight,
Happy Christmas to all, and to all a good night.

Christmas tree in the river at Bourton-on-the-Water.
(Cotswolds Tourism, Cotswolds.com)

ANSWERS TO CUMMINGS' COUNTY QUIZ

ROUND ONE

1. True.
2. Batsford.
3. Just above Slad. It features in *Cider with Rosie*.
4. Bishop's Cleeve.
5. Anne Boleyn, second wife of Henry VIII.
    A field near Sheepscombe is still called Queen's Acre.
6. Daffodil.
7. Bibury.
8. The Speech House.
9. Out.
10. Bertie's Bottom.

ROUND TWO

1. True. The Chief Constable told me this so it must be true.
2. Al Stewart.
3. The gravelly place.
4. Shambles.
5. Bourton-on-the-Water.
6. Tirley.
7. A town.
8. The iconic image of him in front of the Aust Ferry terminal on the front of the album *No Direction Home*.
9. The River Severn and River Wye.
10. He was the first person to surf the Severn bore.

ROUND THREE

1. False. There are no such players but I couldn't resist making the story up.
2. The Regent Arcade in Cheltenham.
3. Butchers.
4. Chipping Campden.
5. He wrote *Thomas the Tank Engine*.
    There is a stained-glass window of Thomas in Rodborough Church.
6. *The Tailor of Gloucester*.
7. 2000.
8. A greyhound track.
9. Fishguard.
10. The Domesday Book.

ROUND FOUR

1. False.
2. The Gloucestershire Warwickshire Railway.
3. Cavendish Square in London. One of the earliest owners of the department store, Thomas Clark, had once owned a small drapery shop close to Cavendish Square.
4. The Crypt School.
5. Cinderford.
6. 99.
7. Imjin Barracks.
8. Northbound.
9. Westonbirt Arboretum.
10. Somerford Keynes.

ROUND FIVE

1. True. I wrote a spoof piece in *Cotswold Life* about stepping on the toes of A-list Cotswold celebrities. Having been asked to open the local fete where Laurence lives I wrote a ridiculous fantasy scenario about him warning me off his patch. 'BBC presenter claims he was kidnapped by Laurence Llewelyn-Bowen' never made it into the paper as we were able to convince them that it wasn't true.
2. A Forest of Dean viewpoint.
3. The Royal Crescent but only just. Built between 1806–1810, it pipped the Pump Rooms by twenty years.
4. Near Wotton-under-Edge.
5. The railway station. It is now a car park.
6. The Promenade in Cheltenham.
7. Lavender.
8. The Butterfly.
9. Rome.
10. Princess Anne. She was doing 93mph on Brockworth Bypass.

ROUND SIX

1. False.
2. *The Rocky Horror Picture Show.*
3. Stow-on-the-Wold.
4. Peregrine falcon.
5. The National Trust.
6. Chocolate crumb, which was transported to Bournville.
7. A town.
8. Smartened up.
9. Allied Rapid Reaction Corps.
10. Olbas Oil.

ROUND SEVEN

1. True. Just one of the many secrets you will learn if you do a guided walking tour of the town.
2. Exeter.
3. The Churn.
4. Barnsley.
5. Cleeve Hill, which is 330m above sea level.
6. The dark-coloured island in the marsh.
7. *This Country*.
8. Longney.
9. Bunch of Nuts, which is on Chalford Hill in the Stroud valleys.
10. Pittville Lake. Local people in Cheltenham raised money for the craft. It was intended for use at Burnham-on-Sea. To show it off, they decided it should have its first launch in a local lake.

ROUND EIGHT

1. False.
2. Dennis Potter.
3. An apple.
4. Sir Thomas Rich's.
5. '... where the wind blows cold'.
6. M48. The M4 takes you over the Prince of Wales Bridge, the second Severn Crossing.
7. 1873.
8. Stroud.
9. Chedworth Roman Villa.
10. Ever Forward.

ROUND NINE

1. You get a point for either true or false. In an article in *The Sun* in 2017, Roger Moore's pal, journalist Chrissy Iley, claims he was once asked in an interview what he would have if he could have anything he wanted. His wish was to ask Mr Wall's to make a choc ice with vanilla inside and put it on a stick. It's a good story that is often repeated, so I had to include it. You decide.
2. Haile Selassie.
3. Frampton on Severn.
4. Severn Area Rescue Association.
5. Cheltenham.
6. The River Windrush.
7. Horse racing.
8. Poets.
9. They are gargoyles on the top of Gloucester Cathedral.
10. Bewick's.

ROUND TEN

1. False, but it is a recurring nightmare of mine having met the late Bluebell.
2. There was an outbreak of foot-and-mouth disease.
3. The Forest of Dean.
4. The Siege of Gloucester.
5. Out.
6. Nature reserves.
7. Lydney's harbour area was strategically important for ship building and the local great oaks were used to provide vessels for the conflict.
8. The Bacon Theatre at Dean Close School.
9. Members of the Beaufort Hunt.
10. Redmarley.

ACKNOWLEDGEMENTS

IT HAS ALWAYS been my dream to write this book about Gloucestershire and I want to thank Nicola Guy, Elizabeth Shaw, Lauren Kent and the team at The History Press for backing that vision and making it happen. Thanks to all my fellow authors for their generosity and help, including Katie Fforde, Caroline Sanderson and Candia McCormack for your sage advice, and David Hanks, David Elder for kindly sharing your brilliant photos. Two local legends I'd like to mention are fellow broadcaster Pete Wilson (thank you for your photos, friendship and fun) and my River Severn guru Chris Witts for introducing me to Sabrina.

Thanks also go to the Gloucester Civic Trust for all your help with the book and for inviting me into your family as an honorary member. I am deeply grateful to Gloucester Town Crier Alan Myatt and the Court Leet of Barton St Mary for years of tomfoolery, endless laughter and the unique material our adventures have provided for this project. I would like to thank Jack Russell for his contribution. He was a great cricketer and now a brilliant artist and it is our shared love for the county that binds us together. Rich Treen plotted the Tour de Gloucestershire route, so blame him when you are struggling up Stanway Hill.

All the local tourism teams have been a great help and also kindly shared many photos. Please use them to help you enjoy this wonderful county. Cotswolds Tourism, www.cotswolds.com; Forest of Dean and Wye Valley Tourism, www.visitdeanwye.co.uk; Visit Cheltenham, marketingcheltenham.co.uk; and Visit Gloucester, www.visitgloucester.co.uk.

My favourite book of all time is *A Literary Tour of Gloucestershire and Bristol*. I spent many happy days with author David Carroll exploring the locations mentioned in his book. This lit a spark in me and I hope you have many happy hours reading and exploring as I did. I could only write this book because of the experiences I have had with the people I have met along the way, so thank you to everyone I have connected with over the last thirty years, including Gloucester Rugby and my friends in the Shed. My final thanks go to the tens of thousands of listeners who have enriched my life, filled me with love and knowledge and provided me with such a unique insight and material for my love letter to Gloucestershire. Enjoy the quiz questions, behave yourself with the Fern Ticket and remember it is now time to squeeze every drop out of Glorious Gloucestershire.

INDEX

ABOUT THE AUTHOR

Mark is an award-winning BBC radio presenter, journalist and writer and has been broadcasting for over forty years. He's presented several West Country travel series for *BBC Points West* and writes a monthly column for *Cotswold Life*, which has been running since 2005.

In 2023, Mark was the recipient of the Outstanding Contribution to the Community Across Gloucestershire Award. He is a season-ticket holder for Gloucester Rugby Club, an honorary member of the Gloucester Civic Trust and former Mock Mayor of Barton (a fun, non-political role dating back to the English Civil War).

Mark lives in the South Cotswolds with his wife, Jo. They have two grown-up daughters, Kate and Ali. Having travelled extensively as a backpacker, now as an empty nester, Mark's writing includes travel features reflecting his love of adventure. As a keen walker, cyclist and campervan owner he shares his experiences in his unique style. To read more about Mark's adventures and where to follow him on social media, visit his website: markcummingsandgoings.com.